RASHI

The Story of
Rabbi Shlomo Yitzchaki

RASHI

The Story of
Rabbi Shlomo Yitzchaki

by
Yaacov Dovid Shulman

CIS
P·U·B·L·I·S·H·E·R·S
New York · London · Jerusalem

Published and distributed
in the U.S., Canada and overseas by
C.I.S. Publishers and Distributors
180 Park Avenue, Lakewood, New Jersey 08701
(908) 905-3000 Fax: (908) 367-6666

Distributed in Israel by
C.I.S. International (Israel)
Rechov Mishkalov 18
Har Nof, Jerusalem
Tel: 02-518-935

Distributed in the U.K. and Europe by
C.I.S. International (U.K.)
89 Craven Park Road
London N15 6AH, England
Tel: 81-809-3723

Book and cover design: Deenee Cohen
Typography: Devorah Rozsansky
Cover painting: James Gain

ISBN 1-56062-215-6 hard cover
1-56062-216-4 soft cover

PRINTED IN THE UNITED STATES OF AMERICA

Table of Contents

Introduction

IT IS WITH AN AWARENESS OF PROFOUND INADEQUACY THAT I HAVE worked on this biography of Rashi.

There have been extraordinary *talmidei chachamim*. But Rashi was unique.

Rashi's greatness has actually been linked to Moshe Rabbeinu. Dovid Hamelech sang, "You have risen to the heights, you have brought back captives." (*Tehillim* 68:19) The Talmud teaches that this verse refers to Moshe Rabbeinu when he went up to Har Sinai to get the Torah. (*Shabbos* 89a) But this verse could also be referring to Rashi. The word "captives," שבי, is the acronym for Rashi's name: Shlomo ben Yitzchak. It is as if the verse were teaching that Moshe rose to Har Sinai and asked G-d to show him each generation and its commentators. And when he saw Rashi, he asked G-d to place Rashi under His special providence, so that Rashi would explain to the people of Israel the Torah that Moshe had received. (*Sefer Rashi*)

The Chasam Sofer quoted the verse, "In every place set aside for My name." (*Malachi* 1:11) "Set aside for My name" is מקטר מגש לשמי –the last letters spell out: Rashi. (*Chut Hameshulash Hachadash*) Rashi was set aside for the sake of G-d's great name.

What was the nature of Rashi's accomplishment?

In the midst of Europe, in the midst of the Middle Ages, there arose a man. He learned Torah, he headed a *yeshivah*, he led a community. He wrote commentaries, *teshuvos* and a handful of *piyutim*. There have been many such *talmidei chachamim* throughout the ages. But Rashi was different. So great was his contribution that his words became accepted as the guidelines for Jews of all communities across the world for all generations.

Almost as soon as Rashi wrote his commentaries, they were accepted by all of Israel as the classical, authentic, unquestioned explanation of the Torah.

He wrote the *peirush* on the *Chumash* that every child and adult learns, often taking it for granted. He wrote the *peirush* that accompanies every phrase that one learns in *Gemara*, as if it were a part of the *Gemara*. He stands at a Jew's side always giving direction, an almost invisible, always-present teacher.

But to recite these facts is still to come up short in attempting to understand the nature of Rashi's accomplishment.

The mystery remains: who was Rashi–ubiquitous and overwhelming, yet so modest and discreet?

Only a man who had the mind of a genius, the heart of a *tzaddik* and the purity of an angel could have attained such greatness.

From Rashi's *teshuvos* and the comments of his students,

we learn something of his life. Folk tales have added a dimension of understanding to Rashi's character; a number of these folk tales are presented in this book, in new reworkings.

Based on such sources, this book provides a popular biography of Rashi. But who could claim that he was capable of understanding even a thousandth of the life of the Teacher of all Israel?

Much of the material on which this book is based was found in *Rashi—Rabbi Shlomo Yitzchaki*, by Rabbi Eliezer Meir Lipschitz.

Other sources include *Heichal Rashi, Kovetz Rashi, Sefer Rashi, Gezeiros Ashkenaz Vetzarfas* and *The Jews and the Crusaders*.

Often, a *halachic* decision that Rashi gave is presented in the form of a dramatization of the problem that he dealt with. This dramatization is usually a work of the imagination.

Any errors or misstatements are my own responsibility, and I would appreciate hearing from readers if they find such.

Just as no book could represent the totality and dimension of the Torah itself, no book can adequately represent who Rashi was and the greatness of his contribution to Torah. Rashi was, indeed, "the brother of the holy Torah." (*Sichos Haran*)

Yaacov Dovid Shulman
Menachem-Av 5753 (1993)

1

Never Give Up Hope

A HORSE CART RATTLED DOWN THE ROAD. THE MAN HOLDING THE loose reins had a thick, rectangular beard and profound, luminous eyes. Behind him, two teenagers gazed at the broad fields through eyes slitted against the blazing sunlight.

The cart trundled past peasant houses and turned onto a bumpy path between two fields. Rows of vines stretched to the horizon.

Rabbi Yitzchak and his two helpers looped cloth bags about their necks and stepped into the long rows of vines, hunting amidst the cascading leaves for the clusters of translucent grapes.

By the end of the day, the floor of the cart was covered with grapes. The two teenagers walked alongside the cart, and Rabbi Yitzchak led the plodding horse by the reins.

A golden haze softened the town walls before them. The

rough stones rose up high, spotted with scrub.

The road ran alongside the Trévois Canal, where geese paddled on the violet water, plunging their heads under the surface to hunt for scraps of food.

At the Croncels Gate, a pair of guards nodded them in.

The streets were barely seven feet wide. Sometimes, a three-story building sagged over the street and leaned against the building on the other side.

They passed the Peter Cathedral and the Abbey of Saint Loup, where monks strolled in the street.

Finally, they came to Rue de la Synagogue and Rue des Juifs.

One of the young men pulled open the heavy door of a small stone house and carried the grapes into the musty room. The room contained vats, scattered barrels and a wine press whose great screw reached six feet up.

The other young man led the horse to a sagging stable. Carpenter bees were climbing in and out of a hole above the lintel of the door.

Rabbi Yitzchak walked up the street to the *beis midrash*. The summer was the busy season. But then there would be the long winter months, when he could devote most of his time to learning Torah. His family had been composed of Torah scholars in an unbroken line of thirty-two generations, leading directly to the great Sage, Rabbi Yochanan Hasandler. He, too, was an accomplished *talmid chacham*.

Rabbi Yitzchak stepped into the *beis midrash*. At a table in the far corner of the room, a middle-aged man sat before a bound manuscript of a Talmud written on parchment. He was teaching five teenagers.

Rabbi Yitzchak immediately recognized the words. The man was teaching the third chapter of *Mesechte Shabbos*. Just as Rabbi Yitzchak had done in his own youth, the students repeated a phrase after the *rebbi*. The *rebbi* gave an explanation of the phrase, and the students repeated this as well. It was more important that the students remember these explanations than the text itself, for they were not written down anywhere, except for the private notes that students took.

Since the completion of the Talmud six hundred years earlier, teachers had added their comments, and these had become a vast oral tradition explaining the meaning of the *Gemara*. Each student repeated these over and over until they were pressed into his memory.

So standard had the comments become that Rabbi Yitzchak mentally repeated the words before the teacher could say them.

Soon Jews began coming in for *Minchah*. Rabbi Yitzchak recognized them all. Altogether, Troyes (pronounced trwä) had a population of ten thousand. Of these, about two hundred were Jews. Because the community was so small, most Jews were related to Rabbi Yitzchak by blood or marriage.

The room filled with men of all professions: bankers, farmers and, like Rabbi Yitzchak, winemakers. There were butchers, merchants, tanners, goldsmiths, silversmiths, shoemakers, glass-makers and barbers.

It was not until after midnight that Rabbi Yitzchak walked down the gloomy street to his house. He could hear the distant steps of his *chavrusa* tapping against the cobblestones. The heavy door to his house creaked open, and he slipped inside.

Candlelight flickered from the dining room.

Rabbi Yitzchak went to the doorway. His wife Miriam stood up to meet him, two long, wooden needles and a length of knitting in her hands. In the light of the beeswax candle on the table, her face was pale and round. A kerchief was tied tightly on her head, even covering her ears.

Rabbi Yitzchak and his wife sat down at the little table, Miriam still holding her knitting in her lap.

Rabbi Yitzchak looked pensive. "The rabbi gave a talk. He spoke about how the greatest rabbis of the last generation are passing away. Last year, Hai Gaon died; the era of the *geonim* is over. And now Rabbeinu Gershom, the great light of Torah, has grown very ill."

The candle flickered in the draft, sending shadows skittering across their faces. "The rabbi reminded us that 'The sun also rises, and the sun goes down.' (*Koheles* 1:5) Our Sages have asked, How can the sun rise before it goes down? But this verse refers to the leaders of the generation. Even before one leader dies, a new leader is born. Who knows? Perhaps in the merit of our own ancestors . . . ?"

His wife gave an involuntary shiver, and Rabbi Yitzchak fell silent. They were a childless couple. But didn't the rabbis teach that G-d's salvation could come in the blink of an eye?

"It's getting late," Rabbi Yitzchak's wife said. She stood up, and he stood as well.

She put her knitting down on the table. Rabbi Yitzchak caught her glance and looked away.

"In the blink of an eye . . ." he murmured.

"What did you say?"

Rabbi Yitzchak picked up the candle-holder. "A saying of our Sages," he said. "We should never give up hope."

He walked through the dark house, followed by his wife. The flame shivered, and shadows leaped about fantastically. It was as though the shadows themselves were dancing to the rhythm of the alluring, promising words, "In the blink of an eye."

2

A Tale of a Jewel

IN THE YEARS TO COME, STORIES WERE HANDED DOWN TELLING OF Rashi's life. Eventually, these were written down and preserved. To what degree they are records of actual fact is impossible to tell. Stories that began as simple narrative may have been embellished over the centuries and transformed into elaborate episodes.

But many of them have joined the unofficial heritage of the Jewish people and become part of a Jewish upbringing. They are a record of the reverence the Jewish people have had for Rashi throughout the centuries.

Perhaps the most famous story is that of Rashi's father and the precious jewel.

"In all your ways, know Him." The verse passed through Rabbi Yitzchak's mind as he looked up from the vineyard at the blazing sun. In the broad, flat landscape that spread out to the horizon, he was an ant under the ray of an infernal magnifying glass.

The sun had shriveled the vine leaves to a dry green. Underneath, the grapes were also pale. Rabbi Yitzchak took hold of a cluster. A caterpillar raised its head. It seemed to be looking at Rabbi Yitzchak in mockery, weaving in his face the mandibles with which it was destroying his crop.

Rabbi Yitzchak twisted off those grapes that were still salvageable and threw them into the bag that lay behind him on the ground. A mile away, the stone walls of Troyes shimmered in the haze. Along the top of the crenelated walls marched sentries, and bright crimson banners hung limply.

There, on Rue des Juifs, Rabbi Yitzchak knew, the young men were learning the words of the holy Torah, which are "our lives and the length of our days." (*Siddur*) But he could not be among them.

Rabbi Yitzchak took a deep swallow from a pitcher of tepid water into which small bits of straw had fallen.

He moved down the row of vines, gnarled and thick as his wrist, held up by lengths of rope that were hung between poles.

The sun had crawled across the sky and was already dipping into the western hemisphere.

Rabbi Yitzchak trundled a wheelbarrow along the ends of the rows, loading on all the grapes until they overflowed. He wheeled the barrow back to a stone hut, into which he dumped the grapes.

Rabbi Yitzchak gave a final look at the grapes and sighed deeply. These would not be enough even to buy fish for *Shabbos*.

Rabbi Yitzchak headed back up the dusty path leading to the main road that would bring him back to Troyes.

Overhead, a flock of geese passed in a straggling V. The

honks of the birds grew fainter until the geese grew as small
as jots of charcoal and disappeared.

He noticed something glittering in the dust.

He bent over and picked up the glistening object. It was
a rock the size of a dove's egg. Rabbi Yitzchak blew the dust
off the rock. It was craggy and dull. Just one small facet was
clear—it was this that had glistened. He held it up to the rays
of the setting sun, and it sparkled, a fountain of rainbows.

Rabbi Yitzchak tucked the stone into the canvas purse
that hung from his belt. Perhaps he could sell it for a franc or
two. Or he could ask Betzalel the jeweler to polish it so that
his wife could wear it as a brooch.

By the time Rabbi Yitzchak entered Troyes, the shadows
were long upon the ground. A cool breeze stirred fitfully, and
a few people were walking to the synagogue for *Minchah*.

After prayers, Rabbi Yitzchak hurried home.

In the small living room, on a plain table, were old, rough
plates. His wife came in from the kitchen, carrying a blackened pot without a handle, using a rag as a pot-holder.

With a wooden spoon, his wife divided the groats and
vegetables into the two plates. "I'm afraid that this is all there
is for supper."

"Thank you. It's more than enough. Look! I brought you
something." He pulled the stone from his purse.

"What is it?"

"I found it on the road. I'll have Betzalel polish it for you."

"Yitzchak, we don't have enough money for *Shabbos*
candles! You can't pay Betzalel—"

Rabbi Yitzchak moved to put the stone back in his purse.
Its clear facet caught the light of the candle and sent out a
burst of delicately-hued miniature columns.

"Yitzchak! This is a precious stone!" A memory flashed in
her mind: she had been a little girl, eight or nine years old. Her
father, a goldsmith, had been working in his shop when she

had come in to watch him.

He had taken a stone from his purse and held it up so that it blazed with light. She had gazed at it, entranced. "Look," he had said. "A precious stone. It will bring at least a hundred francs."

"Yitzchak!" Miriam now said. "Wow! This stone must be worth at least a hundred francs. I'll take it to Betzalel tomorrow."

That night, as Rabbi Yitzchak pulled the cover over him, he heard his wife murmuring as she did every night, and his joy was mixed with sadness. In the corner of the room, she was entreating G-d, "In the merit of our holy forefathers, as You sent children to our mother Rachel and to Channah, Father Who visits the barren with seed, please send children to Your unworthy and humble maidservant."

Early the next morning, Rabbi Yitzchak's wife hurried to the shop of Betzalel the jeweler.

Children were running in the street, and something broke in her heart. She had no son to send off every morning to learn Torah, to come home and recite the *parshah* or the *mishnayos* he had learned. Adjusting her scarf with a nervous gesture, she hurried to the jeweler.

When Miriam arrived at Betzalel's little shop, he was setting an emerald in a ring. He was a gray-bearded man who had been friends with her father.

"My husband found a stone outside the city wall," Miriam said. "I wanted to ask if it is worth anything." She took the stone from her purse and put it on the table.

Betzalel held up the stone and turned it about. When it caught the light and sparkled, he brought his lips together and raised his eyebrows. He brushed the stone with a soft cloth and held it up again, turning it about and examining it with his head tilted to the side.

"Where did you say you found this?"

"My husband found it when he was coming back from the vineyards."

Betzalel looked up at her. "Do you know that this is a precious stone?"

"I thought it might be. My father used to—"

"How much do you think it's worth?"

"I don't know. Maybe a hundred francs. But if you think that's too much, I'll—"

"A hundred francs?" Betzalel put down the stone and laughed softly.

"I'm sorry, I—"

"A stone of this purity and size—once it is cut and polished—what do you say to a hundred thousand francs?"

"A hundred thousand . . . !"

"Congratulations! You and your husband are now the wealthiest Jews in Troyes—in all of Champagne."

Miriam's heart stopped and her heart pounded hard against her chest. "The wealthiest . . . ?"

"If you allow me to hold the stone, I shall cut it and sell it for you."

"I . . . I have to speak with my husband first."

"Of course!" Betzalel put down the jewel, and Miriam slipped it into her purse. "Now you take good care of that!"

Miriam nodded numbly and made her way back home.

Should she wait for her husband? Send him a message? She hid the stone in the little stove and set out to the vineyard.

"Good morning!" Rabbi Yitzchak greeted her. "What are you doing here?"

His wife smiled at him brilliantly. "Good news!"

"Yes? What is it?"

"The stone that you found. Betzalel says it's worth a hundred thousand francs!"

"Blessed be the L-rd!" Rabbi Yitzchak stood still a minute. "But it may belong to someone else. Before we can rest easy that it's ours, I'll have to make an announcement."

In the evening, Rabbi Yitzchak announced his find in the synagogue, and the next morning in the marketplace. But no one claimed the stone.

Betzalel the jeweler had begun hunting for buyers. News of the precious stone carried far and wide—but who could afford to buy it?

Past the mountains, beyond the sea, lived the emperor in a magnificent palace. At the entrance to the palace stood an idol, the marble folds of whose robe seemed to quiver in the wind; and when the sun shone upon the statue's face, its alabaster cheeks glowed like a child's.

Most magnificent of all were the idol's eyes. In its sockets had been placed two precious jewels. When the sunlight shone directly on them at the time of the emperor's morning prayers, they blazed with a glory that cast a pall of terror upon the pilgrims who came to petition the emperor and worship before his idol.

But one day, one of the precious stones disappeared. The emperor had raged and his courtiers had quivered in fear. Only one eye shone with dread majesty, while the hollow socket was a mockery upon its worship.

The emperor sent far and wide to recover the stone or find its like, but in vain. Hopeful candidates brought precious stones of all sizes and colors, but he rejected them all with a disdainful "Faugh!"

Now he had heard of a Rabbi Yitzchak, who possessed a jewel that was fit for the idol.

The emperor swiftly dispatched two messengers to the distant city of Troyes with instructions that they bring Rabbi Yitzchak and his precious stone.

Sailing on a swift barque, the messengers flew across the glassy waves of the limitless sea until they came to the coast. There, they rode upon winding roads through cozy valleys and the passes of mighty mountains whose craggy peaks, covered with snow even in summer, pierced the skies. Fierce winds blew, and the clinging mist made the narrow roads treacherous.

After months of hard travelling, the messengers came in sight of the brave towers of Troyes. Taking off their plumed caps, they bowed and gave thanks to the idol they served for having brought them in safety to their journey's end.

That very day, after obtaining lodging and taking sustenance, the messengers visited Rabbi Yitzchak at his home.

One of the men, Jules by name, with a hard gaze and hair gray as the cold steel of a sword, addressed Rabbi Yitzchak brusquely. "The emperor desires the stone that you possess. He is fair and honorable, for he is the emperor, and he shall pay its full price."

Rabbi Yitzchak and his wife glanced at each other with joy.

"The emperor requests—and his request is his subjects' command—that you accompany us back to his royal palace so that you may have the honor and privilege of seeing the installation of the jewel."

"I shall be most happy to do so."

"That is as it should be. The jewel shall be used to fill the eye socket of the emperor's idol."

"What? I—I don't understand . . ."

The other messenger, a short man with twisted lips named Marcel, interrupted hoarsely. "No need to understand. The emperor wants something done, so it gets done. If you've got a problem with that—maybe there's an accident . . . maybe your little lady . . ." He smiled mirthlessly, revealing two golden teeth.

Rabbi Yitzchak exchanged a frightened glance with his wife. "Yes, I understand. When do we start out?"

Jules replied, "Tomorrow when the rooster crows."

"My dear wife," Rabbi Yitzchak said after the two messengers had departed, "I cannot allow this jewel to be used in the service of idolatry. Nor can I needlessly allow our lives to be placed in jeopardy. With G-d's help, I must find some stratagem by which to elude this misadventure."

After a night of prayer, Rabbi Yitzchak left behind his beloved wife and stepped into the carriage of the two imperial messengers. The horses threw their heads back wildly, the coachman snapped his whip and the carriage rattled through the narrow streets of Troyes, sending children and merchants scattering into doorways.

In a pouch beneath his shirt, Rabbi Yitzchak carried the precious jewel.

He leaned out the narrow window as the carriage clattered past the Jewish quarter. There stood the rabbi of the community, an assembly of his friends and his wife, waving a kerchief.

"Farewell!" Rabbi Yitzchak called out. The breeze whipped the words away from his mouth.

"See you soon!" he heard the desperate, hopeful words from his wife's lips.

The carriage whisked him down the street, and, looking back, he saw for an instant a flickering kerchief.

All through the land journey, Rabbi Yitzchak could not think how he might save himself. They passed through sunny valleys where oxen drew wooden plows over rich, dark soil, where stout farmers in brightly-colored garments sat on horse-drawn wagons overflowing with purple plums and pink-cheeked apricots, where huge wheels of hay stood in shorn fields stretching out gold and auburn.

Then the horses plunged through icy creeks and clambered to the opposite banks, and the farmlands gave way to forest where every evening the ghostly howl of the wolf reverberated through the air. And still Rabbi Yitzchak could not figure out how to solve his predicament.

The road stretched upwards, ever upwards. At times, they would come to a rocky plateau where only flat scrub grew, and Rabbi Yitzchak would see before him the awesome mountains, their massive walls jutting into the eternal fog about their peaks.

Still, the messengers hastened ever onwards, never resting.

They made their way through mountain passes where the cold wind whipped mercilessly, and ice formed on Rabbi Yitzchak's beard and eyelashes. In small inns along the road, rough mountain men would come out and, barely speaking a word, conduct them into unheated rooms where Rabbi Yitzchak would huddle under massive quilts and shiver, his breath blowing white steam into the frigid air.

Finally, they spanned the mountain range and came down again to a forest, which eventually gave way to farmland. Now there was a cool, salty breeze. They were approaching the sea.

Rabbi Yitzchak grew despondent. With every step, he was coming closer to the palace of the emperor—and still, he could think of no plan that would secure his and his wife's safety.

Too quickly, they gained the coast. One morning, after a sleepless night in a hostel that overlooked the wharves, Rabbi Yitzchak and the two messengers boarded a schooner bound for the capital where the emperor made his residence.

The little ship set its prow into the choppy waves, and with a wild cry from the scar-faced captain, the uncouth sailors unfurled the sails, raised the anchor and cast off from shore.

The sea was agitated. Rabbi Yitzchak could barely walk on deck without holding on to the railing, looking at the foam-crested waves smash into the wooden hull and splash onto his legs.

And this, at last, gave Rabbi Yitzchak an idea. It might not work. But he could no longer delay.

Neither he nor the messengers had spoken to the motley crew about the jewel that he was carrying to the emperor. But now Rabbi Yitzchak took the stone from its pouch and began boasting about the great treasure that the emperor had asked him to deliver.

He went up to each sailor and engaged him in conversation. "Look at this stone!" he would exclaim, grasping his rude companion with one hand while he held the jewel up with the other. "Is it not exquisite? The emperor himself has summoned me that I might grace his palace with the splendor of this jewel."

The sailors gazed at the jewel with superstitious awe.

The messengers grew angry at Rabbi Yitzchak, but he acted besotted with pride. "It's my stone that the emperor has requested, and nothing of yours!" he shouted at them. "I'll show the stone to whomever I wish!"

One day, as Rabbi Yitzchak was displaying the stone to the captain, he said, "Look how beautiful! Just see how it shines. Here—take it in your hand and hold it up to the light."

Rabbi Yitzchak held out the stone. The ship trembled, and its prow dipped into a trough. "Oh!" Rabbi Yitzchak slipped and grabbed for the rail. The stone flew out of his hand and sailed out over the water. Desperately, the captain made a grab for it, leaning dangerously far over the rail. But it was too late. The stone flew into the waves and disappeared.

When Rabbi Yitzchak saw this, he howled with despair. In a frenzy, he began tearing at his hair. The two messengers came running to see what caused the commotion.

"Woe is me!" Rabbi Yitzchak moaned. "The stone that I was to give the emperor is gone! My hope for wealth is irretrievably shattered! I have nothing left but to resign myself to despair, for all my grandiose dreams have been cruelly shattered!"

With these and other cries of desperation, Rabbi Yitzchak wandered across the deck half-crazed and disconsolate, until the two messengers took pity. They took him down to his berth, where he lay and muttered in a fever for the next two days.

Within, Rabbi Yitzchak was laughing to himself—yet he was still apprehensive. He had succeeded in getting rid of the stone that the emperor wished to use for idolatrous purposes. Yet would his ruse succeed? If not, he and his wife would be in mortal danger.

When the ship came to shore, the messengers told Rabbi Yitzchak to remain at the coast. They leaped on the back of two imperial chargers and in a cloud of dust galloped down the road to the emperor's royal palace.

The messengers reported how Rabbi Yitzchak had dropped the precious stone into the sea and had almost gone crazy with grief.

The emperor stroked his freshly-shaven chin and declared, "It is a pity. I rue my loss, for this jewel was as precious to me as the apple of my eye. And I feel sorrow for this Jew as well. Send him back home to his native Troyes, where he may live out his life in anonymity, while I continue to lead my influential kingship."

The messengers raced out of the palace to deliver the message to Rabbi Yitzchak.

"The emperor wishes you good fortune on your journey back to your native Champagne." The two messengers left Rabbi Yitzchak at the shore and returned to their domestic functions in the capital city.

Left alone, Rabbi Yitzchak rejoiced before G-d. "Thank You, G-d, for having helped me serve You as the verse says, 'With all your might'—with all your worldly goods. For Your sake, I cast away a jewel that would have made me fabulously wealthy, and I have no regrets. I rejoice in my portion, for You and Your Torah are my portion!"

In this exalted state of mind, Rabbi Yitzchak walked down the streets of the port city, where sailors from all points of the globe sauntered with red kerchiefs about their necks, and porters carried on their backs packages of exotic silks and spices from far-flung cities.

A man grabbed Rabbi Yitzchak by the arm.

"What is it?" Rabbi Yitzchak said.

"You threw away a precious stone in order that you might do the Will of G-d." The man's eyes burned like two coals, and Rabbi Yitzchak drew back in fear, but the hand grasped his arm with an iron tenacity. "By your life, your wife will give you a son by this time next year, and he will be a precious jewel that has no equal in all the world!"

When the stranger finished speaking, he let go of Rabbi Yitzchak's arm and disappeared into the throng. And Rabbi Yitzchak knew that Eliyahu Hanavi had appeared to him.

Rabbi Yitzchak, now alone, made the long, arduous journey back to his city, travelling over the ocean waves that had brought him to this port. Then he travelled along the rolling farms and past broad, lazy rivers that glinted under the sun where sailboats drifted, their nets cast in the shimmering water. At times, he travelled by foot, a gnarled staff in his hand, on roads that led through forests where in the evening owls soared overhead, great wings spread, hunting for the voles that scampered along the forest floor.

At llast, Rabbi Yitzchak returned to his ancestral home.

He flung open the door, and his wife rose to greet him. Two tears that had glistened in her eyes overflowed, shining like precious stones in the dim light.

Then, as Rabbi Yitzchak gratefully ate the humble repast that his wife laid before him, he related to her the story of his adventure overseas.

3

The Birth of Rashi

"MAY G-D BE PRAISED!" RABBI YITZCHAK'S WIFE EXCLAIMED AS HE concluded his tale.

"His goodness endures forever and ever," Rabbi Yitzchak replied. "As for now, despite the emperor's good-will, I do not think it safe to remain here in Troyes. Who knows what new whim might sway him against us, Heaven forbid? We must move to Worms, a few days' journey eastward."

A few days later, they were riding in a wagon filled with their meager possessions. The red, wooden wheels turned clumsily behind the plodding horses. Rabbi Yitzchak held the reins as his wife sat beside him, her hands folded in her lap.

Shinui makom, shinui mazal—when one changes one's place, one changes one's fortune. Perhaps this move would be the means through which Eliyahu's promise would be fulfilled . . .

Worms was a gray, squalid town. The Jews lived on a narrow street where the shadows clung to the walls for almost the entire day.

There, Rabbi Yitzchak and his wife gained the grateful appreciation of the townspeople, for in their innocent piety they stood up against an enemy of the Jews.

There was at that time a Jew-hating bishop who plotted to gain the apostasy of the Jews. Often he could be seen riding down the streets of Worms to the Jewish quarter, his bald skull gleaming fitfully above his tonsure, his black robe flowing down to his heavy shoes.

He would speak in the synagogue, and he would send his priests to preach in the streets and marketplaces. The theme of his talks was always the same: the fanatic persuasion that the conversion of Jews to the Nazarene faith would bring about the Messianic age.

Almost every day, his glistening cranium could be seen wagging in the Jewish quarter of Worms. Among the Jews forced to listen to his words, there were those feeble of resolve and unlearned in reasoning who began to falter in their faith.

Rabbi Yitzchak and his wife gathered the Jews and spoke to them of the simple faith of the Jews, the truth of Torah and the glory of serving G-d. Rabbi Yitzchak spoke to the men and his wife to the women.

The poisonous designs of the bishop were thwarted, and though he gnashed his teeth, the Jews laughed in their sleeves whenever he would preach.

Then Eliyahu's promise received its first confirmation: Rabbi Yitzchak's wife was blessed among the daughters of Israel. Within her began to knit the body of her child.

The months passed, and all Worms rejoiced in the knowledge that she was with child. Every day, she would walk down a narrow lane to pray with the *minyan* that his birth and upbringing should be blessed by G-d.

One morning, she walked to the synagogue, the houses steeped in shadows. For a moment, she walked through a ray of light in which dust motes danced weightlessly. Then she plunged back into the gloom. Even the sound of her steps was swallowed up. A chill damp that had continued for weeks seeped through her bones.

She was walking alongside the brick wall of the synagogue. Soon she would be in the women's section, heated by the feeble wood stove.

There was a rattle, a beating of hooves. Two horses galloped about the turn of the road, pulling a broad wagon. Who was the hooded man who stood on the wagon, shaking the reins violently, yelling at them, "Giyaaah! Haaah!"? Was it ... could it be ...? She seemed to catch a glimpse of a shining expanse of skull. But there was no time to think. The horses were bearing down on her, and the wagon filled the breadth of the alleyway. What would happen to her—and to her baby, who had been promised by Eliyahu Hanavi?

With a cry of prayer, she turned her back to the alley and pressed against the brick wall.

She could see the wild, white eyes of the horses, the spittle upon their mouths, the great hooves that beat at the road, kicking up clods of dirt; behind them, the iron-clad wagon wheel was bearing down on her.

She clutched at the wall. And then—something happened. The wall gave way. She pushed in, grateful, unthinking. The wagon rattled by and rushed out of sight.

Weakly, she pushed her hands against the wall and stepped back. She was astonished at what she saw. The wall had bent in to fit her body, saving her life and that of her unborn child.

Until recent years, people would still point out that depression where this miracle had occurred.

There were those who now pointed in awe at Rabbi

Yitzchak's wife as she walked down the street. Such attention was not pleasing to her and Rabbi Yitzchak.

There were also gentiles who exchanged knowing glances about the miraculous occurrence. "The Jewess is a witch, a practitioner of the foul arts!" Again, the Jew-hating bishop's shiny pate could be seen bobbing among the people of the street.

Rabbi Yitzchak and his wife returned to Troyes, where Rabbi Yitzchak resumed his life as a winemaker.

One dark night, when all slept but the sentries and a few *talmidei chachamim*, Rabbi Yitzchak fell into a strangely binding slumber.

In his dream, Eliyahu Hanavi appeared before him, and announced, "I have been sent by G-d to inform you that your wife will soon bear you a son. Call him Shlomo, for he will be blessed with the wisdom of Shlomo Hamelech and will enlighten the eyes of the Jews in Torah. Guard your wife from any trace of unkosher food, for the child will be holy from birth. On the eighth day after his birth, be careful not to circumcise him until I come and act as *sandek*, for I must give him to drink from the cup of blessing. Then I will bless him that the Torah remain engraved forever upon his heart."

A few weeks later, the child was born.

Eight days passed. Rabbi Yitzchak invited everyone to the *bris*. He himself went to the *mikveh* in the early morning and donned his *Shabbos* garments.

In the hall, the guests sat in their best clothing. Flagons of frothing wine stood upon the table, and loaves of bread, warm and steaming from the oven.

"Just a few minutes more," Rabbi Yitzchak assured the guests as the morning slipped by. "I'm waiting for a few more guests." Where was Eliyahu Hanavi?

The sun slipped over the crest of the sky, and still Rabbi Yitzchak hesitated.

Some of the guests began slipping from the hall. Others pressed him forcefully. Didn't he know the *halachah*? It was already mid-afternoon. Did he intend to wait the entire day?

"Please, honored guests." Rabbi Yitzchak's face was dotted with perspiration. "Bear with me."

But the long hours dragged by, and more guests, angry and scorning Rabbi Yitzchak, left the hall.

The sun was already hanging in the western sky and only a handful of guests, impatient and angry at Rabbi Yitzchak, were left. Humiliated, Rabbi Yitzchak left the hall and ran to the synagogue.

Throwing open the *aron kodesh*, he flung himself before the Torah scrolls and sobbed, "G-d, please keep Your Word that You spoke through Your servant Eliyahu Hanavi, the messenger of the covenant. I know I am not worthy. But may Your compassion be stirred. May You pour out Your great mercy upon me. Please do not let my sins cause Your servant Eliyahu to stay away."

Rabbi Yitzchak washed away his tears and returned to the banquet hall.

Just as he sat down, there was a knock. A servant opened the door to a poor man dressed in grimy clothing.

Rabbi Yitzchak jumped up joyfully. Eliyahu Hanavi! "Come in!" He hurried to the door and brought Eliyahu back to sit next to him.

The guests murmured amongst each other. Who was this beggar that Rabbi Yitzchak was giving so much honor to?

"Bring in the chair of Eliyahu."

When the seat was brought in, Rabbi Yitzchak asked the beggar to sit in it as *sandek*. Again, there was a murmuring. There were rabbis and honored men among them. Why did Rabbi Yitzchak choose this beggar?

The infant was brought in, and with his own hands, Rabbi Yitzchak circumcised him. He filled a chalice of wine, and

Eliyahu Hanavi made the blessing, "Who sanctified the beloved one from the belly."

Before *Birkas Hamazon*, Eliyahu Hanavi stood up and spoke on the *parshah* of the week, *Terumah*. He began by quoting the opening *pasuk* of the *haftorah*, "And G-d gave wisdom to Shlomo." Then he discussed the chapter of *Tehillim*, "A song of ascents by Shlomo: if G-d does not build a house, the builders have toiled upon it in vain." (127:1)

After *Birkas Hamazon*, the mysterious guest blessed Rabbi Yitzchak and the infant and swiftly made his way from the room. The guests, nonplussed at the wisdom that he had demonstrated, attempted to engage him in conversation. One ran after him into the street. But the poor man was nowhere to be seen.

4

Upbringing

SHLOMO WAS A FIRSTBORN SON, A WONDER CHILD. ALTHOUGH HIS
father, Rabbi Yitzchak, worked as a winemaker, he was a well-
known *talmid chacham*.

On his father's side, Shlomo was the thirty-third genera-
tion in a line of *talmidei chachamim* that stretched back to
Rabbi Yochanan Hasandler, a student of Rabbi Akiva. And
Rabbi Yochanan Hasandler was known to be a descendant of
David Hamelech. His mother's brother was the great Rabbi
Shimon Hazaken, community leader of Mainz.

The baby grew. On the street, people looked at him with
affection. Great things were expected of him.

At night, Shlomo was soothed to sleep by the voice of his
mother reciting prayers and phrases from *Tanach*.

One *Shavuos* morning, when Shlomo was a little child, he
was wrapped in the *tallis* of Troyes' *melamed*. Then he was

brought to the synagogue. "Listen!" his father urged him in a whisper as the Torah was being read: the Ten Commandments.

After services were over, Shlomo's father led him to the *melamed's* home together with a few other boys, older than he, where *kiddush* was made. The *melamed* took the boy in his arm. "Look, Shlomo!" He handed him wooden tablets onto which had been carved the first four letters of the alphabet and the *pasuk*, "Moshe taught us the Torah, an inheritance for the congregation of Yaakov" (*Devarim* 23:4) and the first *pasuk* of *Vayikra*. He spread honey on the letters, and the little boy licked them off. "This is the sweetness of Torah . . ."

The teacher pointed to the four letters and read each one, and the boys repeated after him.

The tablets were set aside, and a honey cake was brought in. The flour had been kneaded with oil, milk and honey. On the crust, a *pasuk* had been inscribed. The *melamed* read the words aloud: "He said to me, 'Son of man, feed your belly and fill your insides with this scroll that I give to you.' I ate it, and in my mouth it was sweet like honey." (*Yechezkel* 3:3)

The cake was set aside, and the *melamed* picked up a brightly-colored egg, on which more phrases had been written. He read these as well.

Shlomo and the other, older boys ate the sweet cake and the egg, together with apples, grapes and other fruits, which were thought to increase the boys' ability to understand and remember their learning.

Now they went to the Trévois canal. "The Torah is compared to water," the *melamed* told them. "Just as the water doesn't stop flowing, neither does Torah."

Now Shlomo officially began learning Torah. He learned to read Hebrew, to say the prayers and to learn the *Chumash*, beginning with *Vayikra*.

Each part of the *Tanach* had its own tune: Torah, *Neviim*

and *Kesuvim*, and one was not allowed to switch tunes.

When the boys learned, they were encouraged to sway back and forth, so that their entire bodies would be engaged in the learning.

Every day Shlomo learned with the *melamed*, and soon his father learned with him as well: the weekly *parshah* in *Chumash*, *Mishnayos*, *Gemara* and *Halachah*, translating the words into their native French.

The *melamed* was an expert in the structure of the *Chumash*. He had learned and memorized everything possible about the text: the number of words in each book; the spelling of the words, including unusual spellings that left out or added an extra letter; the phrasing of the *pesukim*; and the cantillation, or *trop*.

This traditional knowledge was known as the "*Mesorah*." It went back directly to the time of the *Gemara*. In those days, there were no widely distributed copies of *Chumash* and *Nach* with the proper vowels and *trop* signs. These men devoted years to their memorization.

The *melamed* also taught *peshat*, or the simple meaning of the words. Eventually, a *melamed's* glossary of these translated words and phrases—*laaz*—was produced, following the order of *Tanach*, and containing about 30,000 words. (The earliest such glossary extant stems from the thirteenth century. The word "*laaz*" is from the phrase in *Tehillim* (114:1), *me'am loez*—"a people of a strange tongue.")

On *Shabbos*, Shlomo would listen in the synagogue to one of the rabbis read from the Torah. Travelling rabbis from the land of Israel were especially expert, never mispronouncing a word or reading a word with the wrong *trop*. Years later, Rashi noted in his commentary (*Berachos* 62a), "the tunes of the cantillation of *Tanach*, whether noted in vowels in the text or sung aloud according to the *trop* . . . [the reader] leads his hand over the musical signs—as I saw among the readers

37

who came from Eretz Yisrael."

Sometimes a *darshan* would come to speak in the syna-gogue. The *darshan* was usually an expert in the *Midrashim* and *Aggadeta* of *Chazal*. Such a visiting *darshan* was treated with the greatest deference, especially when he came from Eretz Yisrael, collecting money on behalf of *talmidei chachamim*.

As a small boy, Shlomo learned that he was the scion of a great family, and he thirsted to learn all of Torah. To deepen his ability to understand *Tanach*, he studied grammar. As he grew older, he concentrated on the *Gemara*.

As he grew, he learned of the great schools of learning in his region: the *geonim* of Lorraine (Lotharingia, or Lothar), whose teachers were both in northern France and, nearby, in the Rhineland cities of Worms, Speyers and Mainz. Lorraine, situated between France and Germany proper, was very much under French influence. The everyday language was French, and Lorraine's barons paid homage to the king of France.

Shlomo also learned of daily life about him. From his father, he learned about vine tending and different types of wine presses.

Troyes had great tanneries, and Shlomo learned how parchment was prepared. He saw smiths soldering iron, artisans engraving metal. He passed shops where weavers embroidered silk with gold and wove intricate figures into their material. He learned about how coins were made.

Troyes was an important commercial center. Merchants came from France, Germany, Flanders, England and Italy. Shlomo learned about ships and tides; about the wondrous city of Venice, whose inhabitants sailed the streets by boat; about a great wall in the distant country of Hungary. He saw jewelry imported from Lucca, Italy, taffeta interwoven with silver, gold buckles, hand-worked belts.

Now when Shlomo learned the *Gemara*, he could understand it better. Did *Chazal* speak of the movements of the tides? He had heard merchants from the coastal regions talk about that. Did a *mishnah* talk about the making of coins? He could understand it that much more clearly, for he himself had seen blacksmiths working before the fire.

In Spain, such *gedolim* as Rabbi Shlomo ibn Gabirol taught in a cosmopolitan atmosphere. But in Troyes, the Jews did not study philosophical treatises or struggle with the relationship between Torah and science. Here, the Jews had a simple faith. They learned only the holy volumes of the Torah.

It was a peaceful age. Jews traded with Christians, hired Christian workers, gave their clothing to Christian tailors to mend and shod their horses in Christian workshops. The Jews wore clothing similar to those of the Christians, spoke the same language as the Christians and gave their children French names.

Then, when Shlomo was still a boy, his father took ill and steadily weakened. It was terribly painful to live through: the weeks Rabbi Yitzchak spent in bed; the prayers; the doctors at his bedside, prescribing useless bromides; the neglected vineyards; the creditors, polite at first, then demanding; the final week of his illness; the rabbis who came to stand at his bedside; his death.

His death. What a loss, to a young boy barely in his teens. Shlomo had so much to learn. His father was his teacher as well, with authentic teachings and traditions from their long family line of *talmidei chachamim*. But now his father was gone.

Together with the death of Shlomo's father came the grinding poverty: the scrimping over pennies, not having coals to warm the house, patching old clothes, scrabbling for leftover vegetables in the marketplace.

Still, the years continued their steady progression. Rabbi Shlomo was now a young man and an extraordinary student of the Torah. When he was seventeen, his mother consulted the rabbis and began looking for a *shidduch*.

That same year, Rabbi Shlomo married. On the morning of the wedding day, he walked to the synagogue accompanied by the *talmidei chachamim* and community leaders of Troyes, with three musicians playing. It had rained earlier in the day, and wisps of mist licked at their legs.

At the synagogue, his bride was waiting for him. The rabbi presented her to him, and then the bystanders joyfully showered them with grains of wheat and small coins.

Now the bride went home, and the women helped her change into her wedding outfit. She put on a silk mantle lined with fur with puffed sleeves.

Meanwhile, Rabbi Shlomo went to the synagogue, and soon his bride returned to the synagogue door. They could hear the musicians playing a lively tune, simple and innocent.

Accompanied by the heads of the community, with the rabbi at his right side, Rabbi Shlomo walked out to his bride and stood at her left. His mother and the bride's mother came before them, and the couple followed the two women back to the center of the synagogue. Here they stood together; here he turned to her and proclaimed, "Behold, you are betrothed to me . . ."

They returned to Rabbi Shlomo's new home for the wedding feast.

That *Shabbos*, in the week of the *sheva brachos*, special songs were inserted into the prayers in honor of the young couple.

His wife had known that he would be leaving for Worms to learn. That was why she had married him—for he would be an outstanding *talmid chacham*.

A short while later, Rabbi Shlomo travelled from Troyes to

Worms, the first time he had left his mother—and his wife. In one hand, he carried a package of his clothing, parchments, quills, his *tefillin*, some coins; in the other, a parcel of food.

"I will visit within half a year," Rabbi Shlomo promised. Like his ancestor's teacher, Rabbi Akiva, the young student was exiling himself from his new wife for the sake of Torah.

Rabbi Shlomo wasn't travelling alone. Two other students were also going to Lorraine—one to Worms together with him, and the other further northward to Mainz.

The trade roads between Champagne and the Rhineland were well-travelled. There was little danger of highway robbers falling upon them as long as they stayed with the wagon of the Jewish merchant with whom they were travelling. He had learned in his youth, and all during the journey, he told the youths of the great rabbis he had met: Rabbi Matisyahu of Chartres and Rabbi Yitzchak ben Menachem, the *gaon* of Orleans, whose sister, Bellet, was known for her piety and whose *minhag* had been mentioned in *halachic* discourse. The merchant had also seen Rashi's uncle, Rabbi Shimon Hazaken.

As the carriage rocked over ruts and stones, the merchant continued talking, and the two other students were lulled into a slumber. Rabbi Shlomo sat listening to the merchant speak, looking down at the iron-bound, wooden wheel turning over the dirt road. Then the merchant fell silent, and Rabbi Shlomo mentally reviewed his learning as the large horse pulled them forward steadily and slowly.

5

Yeshivah Student

Rabbi Shlomo—or, as he came to be known, Rashi—
snapped his head up at the merchant's exclamation. He saw
nothing unusual before him: in the distance, a collection of
houses—a town. Sooty clouds hung low over slate, red roofs.
Farmers were also using the rutted road, and the merchant
pulled his carriage to the side to make way for a wagon filled
with sweet-smelling hay.

Rashi's heart pounded. He was coming at last to the center
of the Torah tradition in the great communities of Lorraine.
These communities had directly inherited the teachings of
Rabbeinu Gershom and his contemporaries. Now he would
learn under *talmidei chachamim* who had sat before Rabbeinu
Gershom.

The merchant continued to talk, but Rashi barely heard

him. They entered the town and the blond horse, its head bowed low, plodded down a narrow street between two-story buildings.

Rashi leaped off the carriage, his bag in his hand. "Which way is the *yeshivah?*"

"We'll go to the inn first, you'll get something to eat," the merchant protested.

"I can do that later," Rashi replied.

The merchant grinned. "Now I know that you're a real student!" He pointed out the directions to the *yeshivah*.

The wagon slowly rolled on and left Rashi alone.

Rashi walked down a narrow road in the direction that the merchant had pointed out. Soon, soon, he would be coming to the *yeshivah* that—together with the *yeshivah* in Mainz—comprised the most important Torah center in all of Germany and France.

Geese squawked about his feet. A farmer wearing the yellow Jewish cap was walking in Rashi's direction.

"Excuse me, is this the way to the *yeshivah?*"

The farmer turned and pointed behind him. "Straight ahead. New student?"

Rashi nodded.

"Best of luck, young man!"

"Thank you."

The man waved his stick, and the fat geese beat their wings and ran ahead on their little legs.

Rashi walked ahead. Outside a *beis midrash*, two students were standing, discussing a passage in the Talmud.

"Excuse me, is this the *yeshivah* . . . ?"

The students glanced at him, at his dusty clothing and the package he was carrying.

"A new student?"

"Yes. My name is Shlomo . . ."

"Welcome! My name is Eliyahu."

"And Yosef," the other student said. They seemed older than him, but not by many years.

They shook hands with Rashi.

"Go inside," Yosef said. "We'll be *davening Minchah* in a few minutes."

The two students returned to their discussion.

Rashi took a deep breath and stepped into the *yeshivah*.

It was exactly what he had dreamed of! Tens of students were engaged in spirited discussions. The sweet words of Torah coursed through Rashi's veins, reviving him after his bone-rattling journey. The *yeshivah* was a handsome, spare building, with large, airy windows. Chandeliers hung down on long cables from the high ceiling, blackened from the usage of years of candle-burning.

At the front of the *beis midrash*, a man with white hair was slowly and carefully sweeping the floor in front of the *aron kodesh*. Rashi caught a glimpse of the man's face. It was serene, holy.

Rashi touched the sleeve of a student who stood at his side. "Who is that?" he asked.

The student followed Rashi's gaze to the front of the *beis midrash*.

"That's the *rosh yeshivah*, Rabbi Yaakov ben Yakar!"

"'Blessed be He Who has given His wisdom to those who fear Him.'" So this was the great *talmid chacham* who had learned directly from Rabbeinu Gershom! "But why is he sweeping . . . ?"

"He does that every week," the student replied. "Did you come to learn here?"

"Yes."

"Welcome. You will quickly find out that our *rosh yeshivah* does everything not for his own honor, but for the sake of Heaven."

Rashi quickly became a dedicated student of Rabbi Yaakov.

Rabbi Yaakov ben Yakar had committed to memory all the traditions of the Oral Torah as they had been passed down over many hundreds of years, and in particular in the schools of Italy and Germany. In the company of Rabbi Eliezer Hagadol, he had learned and taught in Mainz. But several years after the death of Rabbi Eliezer Hagadol, he had moved to Worms and opened a *yeshivah*.

Rabbi Yaakov ben Yakar not only knew by heart great amounts of oral material pertaining to each tractate of the *Gemara*, he was also a master of the methods of the *Gemara's* logic and argument.

This was not the only reason that Rashi sat at his feet. Rabbi Yakar was also "the most modest of all men." In later years, Rashi wrote of the teacher of his youth, "I know that he possessed the finest qualities. Yet he acted like a doorstep that is trodden upon. He made himself an absolute nothing, and refused to take the crown, which would have been fit for him, of propounding new things to his generation." (*Machzor Vitry*)

Rabbi Yaakov ben Yakar said that he did not consider himself a *talmid chacham*. He was merely, he said, a teacher of *Tanach* and *Gemara*, and he refused to deliver *halachic* decisions.

One day, the Jewish community was summoned to meet the governor of Worms.

One of the community leaders came to Rabbi Yaakov to ask him to lead the delegation. "Please, Rabbi. This is a very important meeting, for we have issues to discuss that will affect how the governor treats our community."

"This is not for me."

"Why not, Rabbi? You are our leader."

Rabbi Yaakov ben Yakar shrugged. "I am simply a poor man. You community leaders and merchants who have wealth and know about politics and connections—you use the resources that you have. As for me, all I have is prayer to G-d that He have compassion on His people. You do what you are able to do; and I will do what I am able to do."

There was another story that Rashi had heard about Rabbi Yaakov ben Yakar.

It had taken place before he had come here to Worms, when Rabbi Yitzchak had still been teaching in Mainz.

Rabbi Eliezer and Rabbi Yaakov ben Yakar had gone together to the *shochet*, a tall man with thick upper arms so muscled that they bent away from his chest. His face was covered by a thick, scrubby beard and his features were coarse. But his eyes shone softly.

In the slaughterhouse, he took down his gleaming knife from a hook and handed it to the two rabbis. Each one inspected it, running his thumbnail along the edge.

The slaughterer led out a cow. Tying a rope to its neck, he led the end of the rope through a ring hammered into the ground. He pulled at the rope until he forced the cow down to its knees and its head lay against the ground, and then he quickly tied the rope to an iron pin on the wall.

Taking the cleaver-like knife in his hand, he knelt down and slaughtered the animal with a swift back and forth motion. Instantaneously, the cow died, its legs kicking.

Now he cut open the animal, and the two rabbis inspected its organs.

Rabbi Eliezer Hagadol pointed at something on the cow's lung. "The animal is *treif.*"

Rabbi Yaakov ben Yakar leaned over. "It isn't perfect. But according to what my teachers taught, this flaw is of no importance."

The two rabbis left the slaughterhouse. An hour later, a cart came to their houses and left for each of them half of the slaughtered beast.

Rabbi Eliezer commanded a servant, "Take the carcass and

throw it out. I cannot eat an animal with such a flaw." Two servants dragged the carcass out to the back of the house.

When Rabbi Yaakov ben Yakar heard that Rabbi Eliezer had thrown away his half of the beast, he said, "If such a *talmid chacham* has thrown away his half of this animal, how can I eat of it?"

In his humility, Rabbi Yaakov ben Yakar commanded that his half of the animal also be cast away.

Rashi and the other students recognized Rabbi Yaakov's humility and his aversion to making *halachic* decisions. Yet he was their master, and sometimes they felt that they had to press him to make such a decision!

One day, a Jew came to ask Rabbi Yaakov ben Yakar a question in *halachah*. He was not a *talmid chacham* and not a great businessman. He was a wine merchant who made a decent living.

Rabbi Yaakov ben Yakar turned his attention to the wine merchant. Two of his students, Rashi and another young man, were sitting nearby.

"As you know, Rabbi," the man said, "I buy wine from different dealers, many of them gentile. I always make sure that the *halachah* is strictly kept; the wine is never alone with the gentile, he never moves a barrel unless it is double-sealed, and so on. But this time . . ." The merchant told how something had gone wrong, not that the barrels of wine were definitely unkosher, but perhaps one should be strict. "I myself would prefer to be strict," the man said, "but frankly, Rabbi, six barrels of wine! I can't afford a loss like that. My daughter is getting married . . ." The merchant looked at Rabbi Yaakov ben Yakar.

Rabbi Yaakov kept his head averted. The merchant turned to Rashi and the other student, but they too said nothing.

Rabbi Yaakov ben Yakar shook his head. "A complex issue!"

He stood up. The merchant stood too and looked at him hopefully.

"Wait here." Rabbi Yaakov ben Yakar walked out of the *beis midrash*.

A minute passed, and then another. Rashi and his fellow student looked at each other in puzzlement. What was going on?

"Wait here!" they told the merchant. They hurried out of the *beis midrash*. The street was empty. They hurried down the street and turned a corner. There was their *rosh yeshivah*, slowly walking back and forth.

"*Rebbi!*" The two students caught up with Rabbi Yaakov ben Yakar. "The wine merchant is waiting for your reply!"

Rabbi Yaakov ben Yakar gave a sigh. "It is a responsibility." He turned about and walked slowly back to the *beis midrash*.

The merchant was waiting anxiously in the *beis midrash*.

Rabbi Yaakov ben Yakar came over to him. "Your wine is kosher. Go home in peace, and may you have much joy from your daughter's marriage."

Rashi's fellow students came from the best families of Germany and France. Their fathers and relatives were often international businessmen, travelling all over the world: to Italy, Byzantium, Spain, Persia, Syria and North Africa.

One such colleague was Rabbi Sasson, who later became a well-known *talmid chacham* in Worms.

In their discussions of the *Chumash* and *Gemara*, these students were able to bring to bear what they had heard and seen from their surroundings. They had heard of the unusual customs of exotic peoples all over the globe. They knew about ships and oceans; about the production of coins and iron, wood, leather and cloth. They knew about the preparation of foods, such as oil and wine. They knew about farmers, businessmen, craftsmen, soldiers and sailors. They were familiar with caravans and border crossings. This information enhanced and enriched their understanding of their studies, and Rashi paid heed to what they had to say.

In later years, when writing his commentaries, Rashi often made use of this material.

One morning, Rashi sat in the *beis midrash*, his pen scratching across a square of parchment, writing the comments that Rabbi Yaakov ben Yakar had made during the morning *shiur*.

The other students had also written notes, but mere scrawled comments to which they could later refer.

Rashi dipped his quill into the ink and swiftly wrote his notes, compressed and lucid. From outside the open shutters, small leaves flickered, and a ray of sunlight shone on the page like a benediction. He turned over the parchment and began a new sheet.

Rashi didn't have well-off parents and parents-in-law who would support him while he learned at leisure, acquiring knowledge slowly. He felt driven to amass and record as much Torah knowledge as he could in the years that he had free to spend in *yeshivah*.

As a student, Rashi suffered constant poverty. In later years, he wrote, "I lacked bread and clothing, and I carried about my neck the millstone—the responsibility—of a family. But I continued learning under my teachers."

For the rest of his life, Rashi felt that the pressure of his poverty had prevented him from learning as deeply as he could have done. In later years, he wrote, about a particular question, "I never had the opportunity to discuss with my rabbis the exact and intricate points of this problem. Because of my poor circumstances, I was in a great hurry. I had to rely on studying only the broad outlines and basic principles of most subjects." (*Chofesh Matmonim*)

Line after line, Rashi wrote the comments that he had heard in the *shiur*, comments that went back from his teacher to Rabbeinu Gershom and from him back to the *geonim*, an oral tradition that stemmed from the Sages of the Talmud.

The stiff parchment was expensive. Even the ink was dear. Rashi had to take clear, concise notes, saying as much as possible in a few short words.

He came to a point in the *Gemara* where Rabbi Yaakov ben Yakar had given a brilliant exposition of a complex disagreement over the text. Rashi paused only briefly, then wrote a short note on the text. In a few short words, he referred to this complex discussion, boiling it down to its essence. Someone familiar with the discussion would appreciate the brilliance in Rashi's short comment. Someone who was not, however, would see only what appeared to be a simple explanation of the text.

A few lines later on, Rashi had to describe a farming implement. He paused a moment, and jotted down the word in his native French.

Rashi turned the parchment over and pulled a new sheet to him. He dipped the quill in the violet ink. It was pasty, and he poured water into the inkwell and mixed it.

Rashi would return to Troyes intermittently, and his family began to grow. First his wife bore him a little girl named Yocheved. Two other daughters followed: Miriam and Rochel.

Years passed, and Rashi's notes on the various *mesechtos* and *Tanach* piled up, until he had a stack of parchments.

Rashi's commitment to making extensive notes entailed great sacrifice. Parchment was very expensive, so much so that people could not afford even the most basic *sefarim*. In Troyes, for example, certain "verses were left out of *Mussaf* services, because people didn't know them by heart." (*Machzor Vitry*) Only the cantor had a copy of the *machzor*.

Even *talmidei chachamim* could not find everything they needed. Rabbi Eliezer Hagadol, for instance, was not able to learn *Avodah Zarah*, because there was no copy available to him. (*Teshuvos Chachmei Tzarfas* 84)

A number of years later, when Rashi's grandson, Rabbeinu Tam, received a question from Rabbi Ephraim bar Yitzchak, he replied, "If you send parchment, I shall reply."

Rashi learned under Rabbi Yaakov ben Yakar for six years.

Rabbi Yaakov ben Yakar's influence on Rashi was profound. In his commentaries, Rashi referred to his teacher as "my wise old teacher." In later years, Rashi's grandson reported that Rashi spoke of him as "my teacher of *Gemara* and *Tanach*."

Rashi also referred to Rabbi Yaakov ben Yakar simply as "my teacher." Perhaps this was the highest encomium from one man of simplicity to another.

Rashi absorbed so deeply the style, thought and personality of his great teacher that he intuitively embodied his teacher's point of view. In later years, he wrote, regarding a *halachic* decision of his, "My decision is based on the thought of the great giant in *Gemara*, Rabbi Yaakov ben Yakar. It is true that I didn't hear this particular law directly from him. But my heart, my reasoning and my understanding come from his mouth."

Rabbi Yaakov ben Yakar was Rashi's most important teacher, who in turn transmitted Torah to all the people of Israel for all generations. But Rabbi Yaakov ben Yakar left behind him no works, and even his name is barely known.

Rashi inherited this quality of humility. His writings show a man suffused with the spirit of Torah, a calm, broad, peaceable spirit concerned only with presenting the words of the Torah. Rashi learned from his teacher how to be a clear glass through which the student can learn the Torah directly.

Rashi was twenty-four years old when Rabbi Yaakov died.

Almost nine hundred years later, in 1922, an ancient wall was uncovered in Mainz. One of the stones was a tombstone, on which was engraved "The tombstone of Rabbi Yaakov ben

Yakar, who passed into the Garden of Eden in the year 4824 [1064]."

How had the tombstone been transported from Worms to Mainz and become part of a wall? It is not many years since Jordanian soldiers tore up gravestones from Har Hazeisim and used them as the floors and walls of lavatories. One can similarly imagine peasants of the Middle Ages uprooting gravestones and transporting them to cement them into a wall.

Rashi remained in Worms for a while longer. He became the student of a relative of his, Rabbi Yitzchak ben Eliezer Halevi, who also had a *yeshivah*. Like Rabbi Yaakov ben Yakar, he had been a student of Rabbeinu Gershom, as well as of Rabbi Eliezer Hagadol, and he was now Chief Rabbi of Worms.

Unlike Rabbi Yaakov ben Yakar, Rabbi Yitzchak Halevi was actively involved in communal affairs and management.

Although Rashi remained with Rabbi Yitzchak Halevi for a relatively small amount of time—a year or so—he became a devoted student and remained grateful to him for the rest of his life. In his later writings, Rashi referred to him by such terms as "the great tree," "prince of the pillar," "right-hand colonnade and light of Israel." In turn, Rabbi Yitzchak Halevi wrote back, "The generation in which you are is not orphaned; may those like you increase among the Jews."

Soon, though, Rashi moved to Mainz, only twenty-five miles north of Worms, to learn from another relative of his, Rabbi Yitzchak ben Yehudah. Originally from France, Rabbi Yitzchak had been a student of Rabbeinu Gershom and Rabbi Eliezer Hagadol, as well as a companion of Rabbi Yaakov ben Yakar. Now he was the rabbinic head of Mainz, and one of the leading sages of Lorraine. Students came to learn with him from all parts of Germany and France, and questions were sent to him from distant communities.

The synagogue of Worms was Romanesque, a style that gained the effect of majesty through simplicity. How apropos this was to the character of those who taught and learned there.

When Rashi came into the *beis midrash* for the first time, he was an accomplished *talmid chacham* and the close student of two of the greatest teachers of the generation. But he was filled with a spirit of awe and sanctity. This was where Rabbeinu Gershom himself had lived.

Rashi came to have great affection for his learning here. In later years he described it as, "The *yeshivah* of Mainz, the *yeshivah* of Rabbeinu Gershom, who enlightened the eyes of the exile, whose students all the Jews of the region are."

Rashi grew close to Rabbi Yitzchak ben Yehudah, whom in later years he described as "my teacher in righteousness." In turn, Rabbi Yitzchak ben Yehudah referred to Rashi as "my very gifted colleague . . . my friend and companion."

Like Rabbi Yaakov ben Yakar, Rabbi Yitzchak ben Yehudah had attained the quality of unfeigned modesty. He welcomed discussion, for his purpose was to teach others an authentic sense of Torah, not to force upon them subservience born of fear.

One time, Rashi had the challenge of correcting one of his teachers without shaming him. (When Rashi later wrote about this incident, he did not reveal which teacher this episode involved.)

It was the wedding day of the rabbi's daughter. In the kitchen, frantic preparations were taking place. Servants and maid-servants rushed about, sweaty, sooty, heating ovens, carrying trays of food.

The rabbi himself was busy with a dozen matters: where the *chuppah* would be; a question on a phrase in the *kesubah*; last-minute discussions about the dowry. He stepped into the kitchen, Rashi following him, and glanced quickly into the pots and nodded his approval.

In the yard behind the kitchen, a slaughtered deer, whose venison would be served as the main course, had been cut into quarters and deveined. The rabbi glanced at the deer, his mind taken up with other things. "Good, good."

Rashi, looking over his teacher's shoulder, gave a start. Something wasn't right. How had his teacher missed it? The deer's thighs had only had the fat removed—not, as *halachah* requires, the muscle itself.

Rashi later wrote of the dilemma that he faced at that moment. "My teacher was busy with other matters, and so he didn't notice the omission. And I didn't know what to do. Were I to correct the matter, I would be assuming authority in the presence of my teacher. But if I did not correct it, a transgression would be committed."

Rashi turned to his teacher and asked him, "I have a question in *halachah*."

The teacher turned back to him.

"It is forbidden to eat the thigh muscle of a domesticated animal. But does the same *halachah* apply to a non-domesticated animal, such as a deer?"

"Of course it does." Why was Rashi asking such an obvious question? He looked back down at the deer, and looked again. How could he have not noticed the deer's hindquarters? The entire banquet could have been *treif!* He immediately gave orders to rectify the matter.

There was something else compelling about the *yeshivah* of Mainz. Here Rashi was able to study the manuscripts of Rabbeinu Gershom himself as well as of the school of rabbis to which he belonged: the "commentaries of Mainz."

Rashi studied the texts of the *Gemara* that Rabbeinu Gershom himself had compiled. Every *mesechte* had to be copied by hand, and over the centuries, errors had crept in. Sometimes a copyist didn't pay attention to what he was copying. These could be the easiest types of errors to correct, because they were the most obvious. Sometimes a copyist put into the text a comment that a student had written in the margin. And sometimes a copyist, imagining that he saw an error in the text, changed words around.

At times, this went so far that there were two versions of one work: for instance, there was an *Avos d'Rabbi Nassan* of France, and an *Avos d'Rabbi Nassan* of Eretz Yisrael.

Rabbeinu Gershom had declared a *cherem* against anyone guilty of making arbitrary emendations in the text of the *Gemara*. He then had worked to produce an error-free manuscript. Now Rashi was able to study entire *mesechtos* written in Rabbeinu Gershom's own hand.

Rashi's studies of different copies of the *Gemara* eventually made their mark in his commentaries. For instance, in *Sukkah* 40a, he noted about a certain passage, "Thus is it written in all the manuscripts. I worked hard in my youth to reconcile it with what I had learned from my rabbis, but without any success. However, I then found this reading in a manuscript written by Rabbeinu Gershom ben Yehudah."

Sometimes Rashi was able to understand a *Gemara* by receiving the correct tradition from his rabbi. In *Zevachim* 56a, he noted, "I have emended the text in this way, based on the manuscript of my teacher."

Rashi also studied manuscripts of other writings of *Chazal*. In *Shavuos* 34b, for example, he noted, "This is the way of the *Tanaim*, of the *Sifri* and the *Sifra*." And in *Shavuos* 35a, he noted, "So is it written and punctuated in a corrected, accurate copy of the *Mishnah*."

Rashi became an expert in detecting mistakes in the text. Once, while studying *Arachin* 12b, he realized that the word "three" in the sentence, "These three years of their expulsion by Sancheriv," was an error. But he only kept it in mind, because he had no tradition on the matter. One day, he found a manuscript that in fact left out the word "three." Rashi wrote in his commentary, "Thus did I understand in my heart, and it seemed correct to me, although I had not heard it. Afterwards, I found an ancient, corrected manuscript that had the same thing. I told my rabbis, and they were pleased."

This, though, is small praise of Rashi. He was able to absorb the enormous mass of information that constituted the entire transmitted Torah—*Tanach*, Talmud, *Midrash*, and so on—and the *Geonic* tradition and the teachings of his own rabbis. But that was only the beginning. In his mind, he was able to balance and compare all this material whenever he studied a passage in the Talmud or Torah (or, afterwards, when he was asked to deliver *halachic* decisions). In the great merit of his purity and piety, Rashi was aided from Heaven to always correctly interpret our Sages' intent.

In addition to this, Rashi was given the gift of being able to express himself in an unusually lucid and concise fashion. In a few short words, he could untangle a knot of imprecisions and conflicting opinions.

Now, as a student, he was occupied with gathering the vast material of the Talmud and the comments upon it.

Rabbi Yitzchak ben Yehudah shared with his advanced students the notes he had taken of Rabbeinu Gershom's and Rabbi Eliezer Hagadol's teachings.

The study of such private notes had become an important part of the process of learning Talmud.

As the Jews had spread into exile, the study of the Talmud had come to Italy and France.

Students copied notes for themselves in booklets, known as *kuntresim*.

Soon, other students began to learn from these *kuntresim* and to add comments.

Each *yeshivah* had its own style of learning. The *kuntresim* from one *yeshivah* were studied eagerly by students in other *yeshivos*, in an intellectual ferment of learning.

For a few generations, these *kuntresim* were copied and expanded, with corrections and comments added.

By the time Rabbeinu Gershom was the *rosh yeshivah* of Mainz, *kuntresim* existed in his *yeshivah* on perhaps all of the Talmud.

Although the collection of these *kuntresim* was later published under the name of *Peirush Rabbeinu Gershom*, they were not really authored by him. The *Sefer Haaruch* attributes its authorship to "students." (It was in Italy that this *kuntres* was attributed to Rabbeinu Gershom. In France, it was attributed to Rabbi Elyakum, student of Rashi's teachers, and *rosh yeshivah* in Aspira [Lipschitz].)

Another name given to this work was the *Kuntres Mainz*.

After Rabbeinu Gershom passed away, the *Kuntres Mainz* continued to evolve under the *yeshivah's* leadership by Rabbi Eliezer Hagadol and, following him, Rabbi Yitzchak ben Yehudah.

Rabbi Yitzchak ben Yehudah composed his own comments on several *mesechtos*. These eventually were incorporated into the *Kuntres Mainz*. (For hundreds of years, the Mainz *Kuntres* could not be found. Then part of it, covering nine *mesechtos*, was discovered.)

Rabbi Yaakov ben Yakar had also written *kuntresim* based on the teachings of Rabbeinu Gershom, which Rashi had studied. (These *kuntresim* were eventually lost.)

Rabbi Yitzchak ben Yehudah's students copied into their notebooks the comments of previous *kuntresim*, adding to them the comments that they heard from Rabbi Yitzchak ben Yehudah. These students, Rashi's colleagues, later returned to their communities and used these notes as the basis of their own teaching.

These *yeshivah kuntresim* were unfinished products. There did not exist a complete, edited set of commentaries on the *Gemara*. There still remained unwritten a commentary that would function not only as notes for the *talmid chacham*, but that would guide an intermediate or even new student through the complexities of *Gemara*.

This would be the great work that Rashi would undertake.

One of Rashi's fellow students in the Mainz *yeshivah* was Rabbi Elyakum ben Meshullam. After leaving the *yeshivah*, Rabbi Elyakum returned to his native Aspires, in France, where he headed a *yeshivah*. He brought with him a copy of the Mainz *Kuntres*. This version of *Peirush Rabbeinu Gershom* was attributed to him.

Another student was a young teenager with a brilliant mind named Meir ben Shmuel, with whom Rashi forged a warm friendship.

Here, too, Rabbi Sasson, who had learned with Rashi in Worms, had come to learn.

The *yeshivah* winter *zman* was coming to an end. Rashi looked forward to seeing his family again. His children were growing under the guidance of his beloved wife. And he would be able to visit his aging mother and serve her.

Outside the *beis midrash*, a gray bird alighted on a branch bursting with green sprays of leaves and chirped robustly.

In Troyes, Rashi's mother stood at the window, gazing to the east, where her son was learning. Her pale, wrinkled fingers grasped the window sill. Soon she wouldn't have the strength to manage the workers in the vineyards. Her lips moved, and she prayed into the gusting wind. "Let me see my son again . . ."

6

Back in Troyes

SUNLIGHT BLAZED BEHIND RASHI'S BACK, ILLUMINATING THE WALLS of Troyes. Coming closer, he saw the chipped stones of the wall and the sentry's soiled uniform.

The wind blew up with a rank smell. The merchant he was riding with grumbled, "Those tanneries smell awful!"

Inside the walls of Troyes, Rashi jumped down from the wagon and hurried home. He would have a few months to spend here with his mother, with his wife and daughters, helping with the vineyards. It was good to be back home. But still, there was the pull of the *yeshivah*. Shlomo Hamelech had said in *Koheles*, "He who loves silver shall not be satisfied with silver." (5:9) As Rashi later commented, he who loved Torah would never get his fill of it.

In the hot days, Rashi went into the vineyards to manage the crop. "Let us get up early to the vineyards to see whether the vine has budded..." (*Shir Hashirim* 7:13). And still—there was the sweetness of learning Torah. Rashi later commented that the budding vine was the student of *Tanach*; the vine blossom—that was the student of *Mishnah*; pomegranates—they were the scholars of the *Gemara*, filled with its wisdom and able to impart it to others.

Everything that Rashi saw was a reminder of the study of Torah.

The flowers along the roadside—"For the leader, upon the *shoshanim*, the roses." (*Tehillim* 45:1) Roses, Rashi wrote, were reminiscent of *talmidei chachamim*.

The trees that lined the water canal—"like the forest, which is always verdant, so are the words of Torah." The entire Torah, wrote Rashi, was a garden of delights. "He looks like the Lebanon, wonderful like the cedars"—when one delved into the Torah, Rashi commented, one discovered flowers and fresh branches, ever-blooming, life-filled and life-giving. When one learned Torah, one always found something new and wonderful. (*Shir Hashirim* 5:15)

When Rashi returned in the late afternoon, rock pigeons were fluttering about the rugged crannies of the city wall. "His eyes are like doves beside the brooks of water," Shlomo Hamelech had sung. Who were the doves? They were, so to speak, the eyes of G-d Himself, desirous of those who clung to Him by learning Torah. Like the doves whose eyes look toward their dovecotes, so are G-d's eyes upon the synagogues and *batei midrash*. (*Shir Hashirim* 5:12)

At last, Rashi was in the courtyard of the synagogue, where he washed his face and hands. He drank of the water, and he felt with gratification the cool liquid flow down within him. "I am a wall, and my bosom is like its towers." The synagogues and *batei midrash* too gave nourishment to the Jews with words of Torah. (*Shir Hashirim* 8:10)

During his stay at home, Rashi's ailing mother, who had

managed the vineyard all the years that he had been away, passed away. Rashi was twenty-five years old.

At the cemetery, the cicadas sang exuberantly in the grass.

How could the world continue to turn while Rashi felt his heart inside him break with sorrow?

The week of *shivah* passed. What would Rashi do now? His children were growing, and his wife struggled with poverty. He would have to remain in Troyes a while longer to manage the vineyard. Perhaps he would miss half a year, maybe a year, of learning. Once he had set up the business so that it could run on its own, he would be able to return to Mainz.

But in Heaven it had been decreed that he was no longer to be a student, but a teacher.

Rashi's days were filled with the business of the vineyard: the rows of grapes tended against weeds, insects and crows; the succulent grapes that were gathered under the hot sun; the pressing of the grapes in large presses; the rivulets of rich juice that poured into the vats and the pouring of the juice into barrels, the careful addition of sugar and yeast, the long wait to find out whether the juice had turned into good wine; then the sales, Jews and gentiles coming with their wagons to haul away the heavy barrels. All this stole his time away from the Torah.

But he could still learn when the sun rose high in the sky and it grew too hot to work; and in the evenings, when the cool breeze sifted through the streets of Troyes. Only in the months of planting and harvesting was he overwhelmed with work. In the other months, there was little to do but oversee the slow transformation of grapes into wine, and to sell the sweating barrels.

Soon after his return to Troyes, he was asked to join the *beis din*. At first, he was a junior member. On a document signed by the *beis din* soon after he joined, his name was second, after that of a rabbi named Zerach ben Avraham.

It was also at this time, according to tradition, that he undertook the commitment to write his commentaries. "Thus— כֹּה—shall you tell the house of Yaakov," the verse commanded. (*Shemos* 19:3) He was twenty-five years old, the numerical value of the word, כֹּה.

He also began responding to *halachic* inquiries.

Throughout his life, Rashi felt an unending sense of his rabbis' greatness. This could be seen in his *piskei halachah* and *teshuvos*. He would frequently write, "according to what I have been taught by my teachers," or make such comments as "this is what I learned from my old teacher [Rabbi Yaakov ben Yakar], and I follow [his view]," "I did not have the merit of asking my teacher this, but now, after his death, I have heard that . . ." In one *teshuvah* he wrote, "This is what my heart understands, in line with what I was taught by my teachers."

Regarding his own abilities, Rashi expressed a constant modesty. "It appears to me, and I tend to think . . ." Another time, he wrote, "You have forced me to reply, and so I must . . . But I know that you did not need me." Or, "I am the young one among the older servants . . . I reply like a student speaking to his rabbi, fearing to disagree with you." And "I am not fit to be relied upon in this matter . . . but I tell you my opinion as I was shown from Heaven." (The phrase "as I was shown from Heaven" was a stock phrase meaning, "I could not have thought of this myself; any insight I have was given to me from Heaven.")

In his love of Jews, Rashi was mild in his judgments. In one *teshuvah*, he wrote, "From the day that I have understood the words of the Talmud, my heart has tended after those who permit [this matter]." (*Teshuvos Chachmei Tzarfas* 11). Another time, he protested against those who didn't seek leniency but tended toward strictness: "In my opinion, just as one may not allow what is forbidden, one may not forbid that which is allowed, for the Torah has pity on the money of Jews." (*Pardes*)

Rashi had suffered poverty. He knew what it meant not to have enough to eat, not to have adequate clothing, and to have the burden of supporting a family weigh upon his shoulders. In one case, he wrote, "Let it not be an unimportant matter in your eyes to cause a loss of money to a Jew, for the Torah has compassion for him."

Meanwhile, Rashi's daughters were growing. It was the custom to marry off girls at a young age. It was time to consider finding Yocheved a husband.

Was there anyone in the *yeshivos* that Rashi had learned in who would be fit for his daughter? It had to be someone young but pious, learned and of sterling character.

The candidate he chose was Rabbi Meir ben Shmuel, whom he had befriended in the *yeshivah* in Mainz. He was an outstanding young man who would become an outstanding *talmid chacham*.

The wedding plans were speedily arranged. A few months later, Rashi's beloved Yocheved stood together with Rabbi Meir ben Shmuel.

Not long after the week of *sheva brachos*, Rabbi Meir ben Shmuel took leave of his wife to return to Mainz.

At about this time, it seems, Rabbi Zerach ben Avraham passed away, and Rashi became the leading member of the Troyes *beis din*.

The rabbis of France tended to be very strict in judging whether or not an animal was *treif*, particularly regarding concerns about the lung. As a general rule, animals were slaughtered in gentile abattoirs. Since there was a minimum of loss to a Jew, the rabbis felt that they could take into account the most unlikely suspicion of a problem. As a result, most ritually-slaughtered animals were declared unkosher.

But still, Jews were losing money. So in a bold *halachic* decision, Rashi declared that in most cases, the animals were actually kosher. He wrote that there is no need to worry about unlikely problems—"the judge should only judge on the basis of what he sees before him, and one can rely upon his decision . . . Still, the judge must be very careful and consult with experts in the field." Rashi was not being a maverick, for he was following the *halachic* opinion that he understood his deceased teacher, Rabbi Yaakov ben Yakar, to have held.

Soon afterwards, Rashi's son-in-law, Rabbi Meir ben Shmuel, wrote him a letter telling of a case that was engaging the scholars of the Rhineland. This concerned a sheep whose lung had not been inspected. Some rabbis had declared the animal kosher, and others had declared it *treif*. Among those who had declared it unkosher, Rabbi Meir wrote his father-in-law, were Rashi's two teachers, Rabbi Yitzchak Halevi and Rabbi Yitzchak ben Yehudah.

Rashi was disturbed. If his teachers' opinion stood, the Jews of small communities would be unable to obtain kosher meat. He wrote to his teachers, "I am not challenging your great learning and erudition. But this is Torah, and I must understand . . . If your intent had been to give a ruling to counter the temerity of the butcher [who acted impudently], I would . . . have agreed with you. But if your intention is that this be considered a ruling in *kashrus*, I shall . . . quote you proofs and reasons to be lenient in the matter . . ."

Rashi's teachers responded to Rashi with elaborate replies, defending their position. But Rashi refused to change his position. He wrote in a subsequent letter to his son-in-law, "I, your loved one, am writing you to tell you that I have not and shall not retract my position."

In this way, Rashi expressed his large-heartedness and his great love for the Jewish people.

This exchange did not burn away the ties that bound Rashi

to his teachers. Not only did he send them questions of *halachah*, but they sent questions of *halachah* to him as well. And every letter contained expressions of love and admiration.

In one letter, Rabbi Yitzchak Halevi wrote, "Blessed be our Rock, for our generation has not been orphaned nor left unsaved. He has looked to take care of the poor and despised and placed among us a pillar . . . my beloved, my friend, my comrade, my fellow, my dear, my honored, my great Rashi ben Rabbi Yitzchak, who is close to me. May those like you increase in Israel."

He added, in a wistful tone, "Know that I, your friend, Yitzchak Levi, ask every traveller [from Troyes] how you are faring, and when I hear that you are doing well, I rejoice."

Rashi's other teacher, Rabbi Yitzchak ben Yehudah, wrote to him, "You who are beloved above and below; you who rule over the upper and lower hidden treasures of the king; you who investigate hidden matters; you who uproot mountains and shatter boulders . . . [Your teachings] teach the sun in the east to shine . . . You are my friend, close to me, Rashi ben Rabbi Yitzchak, whose name signifies peace. So may it be the will of the Master of peace to reach out to you like a river of peace, like a brook that never fails, to give you the blessings that you desire and that are desired by me, Yitzchak ben Yehudah." (*Chofesh Matmonim*)

7

The Marriage of Yocheved

YELLOW BUTTERCUPS WAGGED THEIR HEADS AMIDST VIOLET anemones, bluebells and tough cylinders of grass with heavy, ridged bulbs at their ends that drooped over.

Rashi continued managing his vineyard. If he did not work, how would he eat? One did not receive a salary for being a *rav*.

Rashi remained in this occupation throughout his life. In later years, he once wrote a letter, apologizing for his curtness. "All the Jews are at the moment busy in the vineyards."

In another letter, he described to his son-in-law, Rabbi Meir, how the wine press operated after some changes had been made in its installation.

Rashi continued to serve on the *beis din* and to write *teshuvos*. Then, when he was about thirty years old, he opened a *yeshivah*.

People began to talk about the great Rashi, the *talmid chacham* of Troyes who had no sons. His daughters, it was said, were unusually pious and learned. His oldest, Yocheved, had merited to marry a saintly, brilliant man, Rabbi Meir ben Shmuel. How had the match been made? Tales began to circulate. As women spun wool they spun stories as well, and these were repeated on late Friday nights when the *Shabbos* candles guttered and the shadows danced.

Here is a tale that was told for generations, a story springing from the genius of the Jewish folk.

Yocheved shook her head. "No, Papa. I don't think I want to marry him."

Rashi and his wife exchanged a look of concern. "He's an outstanding young man," Rashi said.

"I know, Papa, but . . ."

"But what, dear child?"

"I—oh, I don't know!"

Rashi sighed. "You are already fifteen years old, Yocheved. You're not a little girl any more."

"Oh, Papa—I don't want to hurt you—but I just couldn't say yes!"

"It's all right, Yocheved," her mother said to her. "When I was your age, I also didn't know what I wanted."

"But I do know what I want," said Yocheved.

"And what is that, my child?" asked Rashi.

"I want someone—someone as great as you!"

"You will marry a great *talmid chacham*," Yocheved's mother soothed her. "I am sure of it. But remember: even a *talmid chacham* is a human being."

"What do you mean?"

"I mean that maybe you have unrealistically high standards."

"But Mama!" Yocheved said. "When it comes to Torah, how could I not want high standards?"

"Perhaps there is no one who could meet your conditions," Rashi suggested.

"I am sure there is someone," Yocheved said. "There must be!"

Yocheved's mother took hold of her hand. "Please do not be upset that your father and I speak to you this way. We do not want to see a wonderful girl like you become an old maid, Heaven forbid."

"I know you mean well, Mama." Yocheved squeezed her mother's hand.

Two weeks later, a student with a reputation of being a clever and talented student came to Troyes. He was jauntily dressed and his clothes hung well on his lean figure. One evening, Rashi, his *rosh yeshivah*, invited him for a *Shabbos* meal. At the table, wisdom flowed from the student's lips, and his manners were exquisite.

At the end of the meal, as the *Shabbos* candles faded away, the student patted his lips with a silken kerchief that he then tucked into a frilly sleeve. Bowing gracefully, he took his leave of Rashi with great civility and praised Rashi's wife upon the excellent quality of her cooking.

As the door closed behind him, Rashi and his wife turned to Yocheved.

She turned to them with a look of anguish. "Papa, Mama— I know that he is a fine young man. But—please forgive me— I don't know why, but I can't—" She buried her face in her hands and sobbed.

"Now, now," Yocheved's mother came up to her and put her arm about the girl's shoulder. "Don't cry."

Rashi stepped forward. "Tell us," he said. "What is the matter?"

Yocheved looked up at her father. "I know that he is a fine *talmid chacham*, Papa. I'm sorry to hurt you. But—I just can't say yes . . ."

"My dear," Rashi said. "You have turned away many *shidduchim*. Soon, no one will want to marry you any more. Maybe you are being too picky. The Jews are a wonderful people. I believe that even if you were married to a simple Jew, you could be happy."

"Forgive me, Papa," said Yocheved. "But my dream is to marry the greatest *talmid chacham*."

"My dear daughter," said Rashi. "You do not know what will make your life happy and what will make it bitter. For your own sake, Yocheved, I hereby take an oath that the first man who enters this house tomorrow morning will be the man whom you marry."

"Oh, Father!" Yocheved cried. Rashi gazed at his daughter with love and sadness in his eyes.

Yocheved turned suddenly and ran to her room. Throwing herself on her bed, she buried her head in the paisley quilt and sobbed.

Early the following day, Yocheved gasped when she looked out her window. Coming up the lane was a ragged, crooked beggar with a bandage tied across his forehead. Yocheved flung her shutters wide open. "Wait outside," she cried out, "and I'll bring you something to eat!"

But the man merely smiled at her distractedly and continued up the walk.

When Rashi opened the door to the stranger, his face turned ashen, but he asked the man to come in. Yocheved's mother came in from the kitchen to see who it might be, and she too stood stricken, holding a plate in one hand and a hand towel in the other.

Rashi turned to his wife with a faltering voice. "We have a guest. Why don't you put out some food?"

Rashi ran upstairs to his daughter's room. He could tell from her chalky face that she had seen the man.

"Father," Yocheved pleaded, "take back your vow. I'll

marry anyone you choose for me. But don't make me marry this man."

"It is not so easy to nullify a vow," Rashi replied. "But I shall try to teach this man Torah. Perhaps he can still be taught."

Rashi and his wife took in the stranger as a boarder. They clothed, cleaned and fed him, and every day, Rashi sat with him and tried to teach him Torah. But it seemed that nothing could penetrate the man's head. *Alef, beis, gimmel, daled.* He would follow Rashi's finger on the page, repeat their names, and then completely forget what Rashi had said.

"It's no use!" Yocheved said to her father one night before she went to bed. "The man is feeble-minded!"

"A vow is not an easy thing to nullify," Rashi answered her. "Please give me one more chance."

"Very well, Father."

The next morning, Rashi spent another hour again trying to teach the stranger the alphabet and some basic words in *Lashon Kodesh*, but in vain. He all but gave up on the stranger and returned to his own learning. As Rashi learned aloud, he came to a problem in the *Gemara* that baffled him. However hard he tried, the solution stubbornly eluded him.

In frustration, Rashi got up from his learning to take care of other affairs. When he returned that evening and opened up his *Gemara*, a folded scrap of paper slipped into his lap. "What's this?" Rashi was about to cast it aside when he saw that the inside of the page was written on with a careful, neat hand. "A wonderful handwriting!" Rashi marvelled. "The writer of this note is obviously good-hearted and well-learned." As Rashi perused the note, he was astounded to discover a flawlessly brilliant solution to the problem that had so exercised him that morning. Who wrote this? he wondered. Could it be . . . ? No, it couldn't . . . But it must . . .

Rashi called Yocheved down and explained the situation to her. "Oh," she exclaimed, "if this man is as you say, a

modest *talmid chacham* who has determined to conceal his
identity, then I shall most willingly marry him—if he will have
me."

Rashi summoned the beggar and held the note out. "Tell
me, sir, are you the author of this communication?"

The beggar looked abashed. "I cannot deny it."

"Then you are a *talmid chacham* of the very first rank! Tell
me, what is your name?"

"I am called Meir ben Shmuel."

"Rabbi Meir," Rashi said, "I would like to offer to you the
hand of my daughter Yocheved in holy matrimony."

Rabbi Meir inclined his head graciously. "Rabbi Shlomo, I
would be honored to wed your daughter, a young woman of
the finest qualities, and thus to be joined by marriage to you
and your illustrious family."

Rashi shook the man's hand joyfully and called his wife,
who rejoiced with them, bringing them cake and a bottle of
cognac.

And so were stories told about the figure of Rashi, trans-
forming him into a legendary character.

In his *yeshivah*, Rashi began compiling the notes that he
had taken as a student, clarifying and adding to them. These
became his vast commentaries on *Gemara* and on the
Chumash and *Nach*.

These writings were wonderful commentaries, enclosing
within their scope the wisdom of the entire Torah tradition.

They were more miraculous than any tale of miracles.
They were more marvelous than the most enchanting folk
tale.

To these writings, Rashi appended his name as Shlomo
Yitzchaki, attaching his father's name to his. No one else
would refer to him without adding the title, Rabbi: Rabbi
Shlomo Yitzchaki, whose acronym is Rashi.

The Chida wrote that he had found an old manuscript that

explained that if Rashi had been referred to only by his own name, the acronym for Rashi would be Rash, which means "poor." Thus the *yud* of Yitzchak was added. (This would not explain why this was not a concern in the case of the *Baal Tosefos*, Rabbi Shimshon of Sens, who is in fact known as the Rash.)

Sometime afterward, someone discovered that the acronym Rashi could also read, Rabban Shel Yisrael: the teacher of Israel. He could be given no more fitting title.

8

The Winemaker's Tale

A JEW IN A FADED CLOAK SAT IN THE ANTECHAMBER OF RABBI Shlomo's *yeshivah*.

"Excuse me." He stood up and grasped the sleeve of a student who was going into the *beis midrash*.

The student looked at him. He was a simple-looking man, his face seamed and swarthy with the sun. It was obvious that he was wearing his *Shabbos* suit. "I wish to ask the *rosh yeshivah* a question."

The student nodded. "Are you a winemaker?"

"Yes, how did you know?"

The student merely smiled. "Wait here."

So many Jews worked with wine-making. Sooner or later, they would encounter a problem with *yayin nesech*—wine handled by a non-Jew.

The winemaker stood right outside the door, wringing his

cap in his large hands.

"The rabbi will see you now."

"Thank you!" He followed the student into the cool *beis midrash*, so dark after the blazing light of the sun. The student led him past tables where young men swayed, learning in a sweet sing-song.

"In here." The student had paused at a door. The Jew awkwardly put his cap on his head and knocked softly.

"Go in," the student said.

In the small room sat Rabbi Shlomo, the *rosh yeshivah*. The Jew didn't know what to do with his hands.

Rabbi Shlomo regarded him. "Your question?"

The Jew coughed. "If I am not troubling you . . . ?"

Rashi gazed at him benignly.

"Rabbi, this is my problem. It took place last week. You remember the great storm . . . ?"

Rashi nodded.

The Jew shivered, as though he were again living through that night. "Oh, it was terrible! I was out on the road with three barrels of my best wine in my carriage. The driving wind shrieked wildly and tore through the tree branches. The rain hammered down upon my head. Jagged streaks of lightning split the sky, lighting up the night. Then the thunder would smash, and my horses would rear up in terror."

The Jew halted and cleared his throat. "I lashed my horses furiously, eager to reach an inn where I could warm my sodden bones and stretch my clammy feet before the fire." He looked down at his shoes. The soft leather was a shapeless mass.

The Jew sighed. "In the pitch-black night, the wind howled like the wicked on the Day of Judgment. I cried to G-d, 'Deliver me in peace!' But suddenly my horses neighed, reared wildly and dashed into the brush that lined the road. I raised my voice, but the wild wind scattered it away.

"I grabbed the reins to pull the erring horses back. But they struggled furiously and pitched me off the wagon. I heard the heavy wine barrels splashing in the mud, and I myself was mired.

"There was a flash of lightning; in the glare, I saw two peasants coming to me on the road, leading a donkey upon whose sagging back was laden a burlap filled with soggy grain.

"One of the peasants leaped forward and grabbed the harness of my horses, dragging the frenzied animals to order. He held their reins and spoke so softly that, as though bewitched, they stood at peace. The other peasant, tall, with massive arms, hurried to the ditch. There, with more than human strength, he grasped a barrel in his great hands—then, bidding that I stand aside, cast the keg upon the wagon. And then this more than natural giant turned again and raised the other precious barrels from the mud."

The Jew wiped his brow. "Then, as I stammered my thanks, the peasants tipped their rain-drenched caps and disappeared behind their plodding donkey, leaving me to ride the murky road alone, marvelling that G-d should be so good and send me men of such quality."

He sighed. "But when, the following day, I told my fellows of this wondrous night, they said that since my barrels had been carried by a gentile, I must forego the profit on which I had relied to feed my family these winter months."

The Jew looked into Rashi's eyes. "Please do not think me weak if tears stain my eyes and course upon my faded cheeks. If I cannot sell this wine, I must, like beggars on the highway, trod the dust."

Outside the room, the student stood pressed against the door, eager to hear Rashi's decision.

"Please step outside. Ask my student to come in here."

The winemaker stepped out. "The *rosh yeshivah* wants you."

Rashi gestured to his student. "Please close the door. This man has a question about *yayin nesech*. It isn't in my heart to cause a Jew a loss—nor, for that matter, to forbid him to profit even from wine owned by gentiles. After all, in our day and age, they don't pour out wine for idol worship. But I would prefer not to tell that to the winemaker. If news of my position is spread, light-minded people will become too lenient about the *halachos*. (*Haoraah* 1:113)

"But certainly, no one today has seen or heard of any gentile actually splashing wine in idolatrous ceremonies. And we do have a principle that the Torah is caring regarding a Jew's possible financial loss. (*Teshuvos Rashi*)

"So go tell the Jew that . . ."

Rashi instructed his student how to speak to the Jew in a way that would not lead him to misinterpret what he had heard.

The student cleared his throat. "Since the rabbi is already speaking about this matter, I would like to ask him a question."

"Please do."

"A few days ago, while I was holding a pitcher of wine in my hand, a gentile knocked against the pitcher and with his garment and body jostled it so that he knocked some wine onto the ground."

Rashi smiled. "That which spilled onto the ground is forbidden. But that which remained in the pitcher is allowed." (*Haoraah* 1:113)

9

The Commentary on the Talmud

AS A STUDENT, RASHI HAD TAKEN EXTENSIVE NOTES ON THE TALMUD. Now he was a *rosh yeshivah*. It was his responsibility to share his learning and his insights with his students.

And so as Rashi continued to learn, he revised and clarified his original notes. This itself was a mark of Rashi's humility. Although he was now a *rosh yeshivah*, he returned to the notes that he had made as a student. Furthermore, he could have simply given the original notes to his own students. Yet for his students' sake, he was willing to take time from his own learning in order to sharpen the language of his comments.

Eventually, by the end of his life, Rashi revised almost the entirety of his massive commentary on the Talmud three times.

In their explanations of the Talmud, other *talmidei chachamim* had provided many outlines of the Talmud's arguments. Rashi did not follow this path. He preferred instead to comment on the text phrase by phrase.

Part of Rashi's genius was that he made the complex seem simple. Were there two *sugyas* that seemed to contradict one another? Were there two *geonim* who interpreted a *sugya* differently? With a short phrase, with one word, Rashi indicated the way that the Talmud should be understood. Later commentators, such as the Baalei Tosefos, spent hundreds and thousands of words discussing a single phrase that Rashi had written.

Rashi forged a simple path through the great sea of the Talmud where a student might before have gotten irretrievably lost. But when one examines the path, one sees that it is not simple at all. Rather, it is the brilliant amalgam of the sum of knowledge of the entire Torah tradition applied to every phrase in the Talmud.

The greatness of Rashi's commentary is not contained within its words. The whole is greater than the sum of its parts. The commentary is an entity that can be studied in depth, layer after layer.

A blade of grass, by analogy, can be reduced to its cells, the parts of the cells, the molecules of which they are composed, the atoms of which the molecules are composed, the subatomic particles. Then various processes of the blade of grass can be studied. It can be studied as part of a greater ecology. One blade of grass can take a lifetime of learning. And the more one studies it, the more does one come to realize how much one does not understand, and the more does one appreciate the greatness of G-d, Who made that blade of grass.

Similarly, the more deeply one learns Torah, the more depth and layers does one uncover; the more correspondences and connections one reveals. The Torah, it becomes apparent, is an extraordinarily complex, multi-faceted and profound teaching that one could spend one's whole life studying and still only grasp a small portion of. And from the appreciation of the depth of the Torah, one can begin to appreciate the greatness of G-d, Who gave the Torah.

In his commentary, Rashi grasped the infinite greatness of the Talmud. And although seemingly simple, his words too took on the characteristics of the Talmud. Rashi's words too have an infinite complexity and depth.

But like anything else that exists in the world, Rashi's commentary is based in part on the use of certain approaches and techniques that can be readily appreciated. However, to recognize what these techniques are is not to understand the greatness of Rashi's work. By knowing what types of brushstroke Rembrandt employed in his *Portrait of a Rabbi*, for example, one does not yet appreciate Rembrandt's genius. Yet such details can be of interest, and some will be mentioned here.

Rashi made sure always to note where the copies of the *Gemara* that were widespread in his time had an incorrect reading. For instance, in *Chulin* 74b, he commented, "Although these words are in all the manuscripts, in truth it is a mistake. No sage could make sense of this. Due to someone's haste, this error occurred."

Rashi was circumspect in his approach to proposing a textual error. If he found two sources that seemed contradictory, he would note the fact without taking sides. For instance, he noted in *Chagigah* 19b, "I cannot make sense of the language in the manuscripts. If they are right, then there is an internal contradiction in the statements. And why should you prefer to follow the second reading?"

Sometimes, even though he would reject a reading, he would explain the reading in implied acknowledgment of those who did not reject it. In *Chulin* 4a, he commented about a phrase, "We do not read this. But as for those who do, this is the explanation . . ." Similarly, he noted in *Zevachim*

115b, "It seems to me that the manuscripts left something out here, though I don't know what. But if the manuscript is actually complete, this is what it means . . ."

Sometimes Rashi specifically blamed an error on copyists. In *Kerisos* 4a, he commented, "This reading in the manuscripts is mistaken, due to mistaken commentators who weren't expert in the topic and whose misunderstanding affected their reading."

In another case, a student had made a note in the margin of his *Gemara*, which a copyist had then accidentally inserted into the body of the *Gemara* itself. Rashi commented, "We do not read this. A mistaken student who had a question wrote this on his manuscript . . . and the copyists wrote it in the *Gemara*."

Sometimes, if there were two contradictory readings in the *Gemara*, Rashi would point out which one is correct. For instance, in *Zevachim* 120a, he wrote, "This is the reading in *Meelah*, and so should it be here." He would study parallel readings in *Tosefta*, the *Talmud Yerushalmi*, *Midrash* and *Targumim*.

Sometimes, Rashi made use of the writings of the *geonim* to determine a correct reading. In *Shabbos* 135, he noted, "This is how the matter is stated in the *She'iltos* of Rabbi Achai." In *Makkos* 9b, Rashi wrote, "A person who hated [his victim] doesn't go into exile. I found this version in the *teshuvos* of the *geonim*." Or: "I saw in the *teshuvos* of the *geonim* that they would wear [felt shoes] under their [regular] shoes." (*Beitzah* 15a)

At times, Rashi would make a comment based on his feel for the text. In *Arachin* 17b, he noted, "I heard it as it is written in the manuscripts, and the explanation is as I have stated. But this is not the approach of the *Gemara*."

Another tool that Rashi used to make his commentary easily understandable was the use of his native French to translate difficult Hebrew or Aramaic words. These words were referred to as "*laaz*."

The word "*laaz*" was used to refer to the translation of words and phrases into the languages that evolved from Latin: Italian, Provençal, Spanish and French. Altogether, Rashi used about 2200 such terms in his commentary on the *Gemara*. (In later years, copyists, no longer understanding these words, sometimes left them out or mangled them.)

Incidentally, philologists find Rashi's *laazim* valuable for the study of Old French, for he mentions words that are not found anywhere else.

Rashi described many details of daily life that the *Gemara* referred to: how things were manufactured; people's customs; how various tools were used; information about trades and professions; and so on. Often, he would make mention of something his students would be familiar with in order to explain what the *Gemara* was talking about. For instance, in explaining a phrase in *Sotah* 49b, he commented, "This is similar to an arch made of wooden circles, as we now use for hanging up scarves and gold-embroidered veils."

He described various types of furniture and food dishes.

Rashi was able to provide exact details on wine production, such as how wine is siphoned from one barrel to another. (*Avodah Zarah* 72b)

He discussed the workings of an *arak*—a water clock (*Eruvin* 104a) and described a water scale (*Shabbos* 80b). He described mechanical scales, such as the *arsah* (*Shabbos* 60a), and discussed solar power: "water-filled vessels used to concentrate the sun's heat." (*Beitzah* 33a).In describing an invalid *esrog*, Rashi compared it to the watermills of his day: "It has the shape of a watermill wheel." (*Sukkah* 36b)

Rashi witnessed goldsmiths at work, and commented, "They beat alternately three times on the foil and once on the anvil to smooth the mallet so that it would not break the foil.

I have also seen those who mint coins doing this in our place."
(*Shabbos* 103a)

Sometimes he did not view a manufacturing process but talked with the craftsmen. After explaining the making of a glass vessel, he added, "This is what I have heard from artisans." (*Sanhedrin* 91a)

In discussing the *hari* baskets in the dream of Pharaoh's baker, Rashi said, "They are baskets woven of peeled willows. There are many of these in our country; they are used by vendors of fancy rolls." (*Bereishis* 40:16)

Another tool Rashi used to make the *Gemara* easily understandable was to occasionally identify the authorities in the discussion. He might tell who is a *Tanna* and who an *Amora*, the order of the generations, who was the teacher and who the disciple, and where they lived.

Also, if a topic is discussed in passing, Rashi would explain it and refer the student to the place in the *Gemara* where it was fully dealt with.

Rashi also helped the student with the flow of the *Gemara*. Since there are no punctuation marks, Rashi added such remarks as "This is a question"; "he repeats this in agreement"; "he says this in surprise"; "stated in amazement"; and so on.

Another tool Rashi used was to address a possible question a student might have by adding a few terse words to explain the text, without any reference to the question. He also assured the student that a present question would be eventually dealt with: "This will be explained in the *Gemara*"; "it will be discussed further on"; "there is an obvious objection, which the *Gemara* will raise."

Rashi sought the true meaning of the Talmud, no matter how plain, and rejected other interpretations. In *Pesachim* 19a, he commented on another interpretation, "It is very deep, but not defensible." Elsewhere, he commented on someone's explanation, "This is a mistaken comment from a very clever, sharp-witted individual." (*Chulin* 81a) Some people, he wrote, "because of their *pilpul* have forgotten what the *halachah* is." (*Temurah* 15b)

In some ways, Rashi's monumental work was the redaction of five hundred years of oral commentary on the *Gemara*. This would explain the striking similarity between certain of his comments and those found in *Sefer Haaruch* of Rashi's contemporary in Rome, Rabbi Nassan ben Yechiel.

With exquisite expertise, using a minimum of words, Rashi transmitted in an easily-understandable form the wisdom and knowledge of generations.

Almost always, the tradition that he gave over was authoritative. Only occasionally would there be the possibility of more than one explanation of a passage. Then he would write, "I heard this from my teachers"; "here my teacher interpreted this phrase in this way . . . but elsewhere he interpreted it another way"; "this is the wording of Rabbi Yitzchak ben Menachem, but my teachers worded it otherwise."

When Rashi wrote an insight based primarily on his own understanding, he commented, "This is my explanation, based on my own understanding." (*Gittin* 33a)

Sometimes Rashi would disagree with an explanation he had heard. "*Michtav* refers to engraving and forming. This is what I heard. But to me it seems that *k'sav* refers to the form and *michtav* to the pen and stylus." (*Pesachim* 54a)

Occasionally, he questioned his teachers' explanations: "This is the language of my teachers, but I question it." (*Shabbos* 92b); "this is how it appears to me, and I am surprised at the explanation of my teachers." (*Shabbos* 101b)

Rashi worked on his commentary to the *Gemara* until the last years of his life, constantly making it clearer and more easily understandable.

Now, any student who had learned for a while under a

teacher could continue to study the rest of the *Gemara* on his own. The *Gemara*, whose cryptic language had made it a sealed work to all those outside the *yeshivah*, could be studied even by those who were not full-time students.

But in a sense, this is the least of praise for Rashi's commentary on the Talmud. At the same time that the commentary serves as a basic explanation of the text, it is also the most profound, advanced commentary for the greatest *talmidei chachamim*. The *talmid chacham* knows that Rashi's simplest comment needs study. Like the honeycomb hidden within the tree, hidden within Rashi's simple words are sweet depths of Torah that revive the soul.

In later years, Menachem ben Zerach wrote in the introduction to his *Tzeidah Laderech*, "Without Rashi, the Talmud would have been forgotten in Israel." The Talmud would have remained a closed book to the Jews. (Yitzchak ben Sheshes, *Sheilos Uteshuvos Rivash*)

One cannot conceive of learning Talmud without the commentary of Rashi. The merit of every Jew learning Talmud, on whatever level, goes back to Rashi. Rashi walks hand-in-hand with our Sages, and he walks hand-in-hand with every person who sits down to learn the Talmud.

— 10 —

The Tragic Marriage

IN THE *BEIS MIDRASH*, THE MEN WERE SINGING A TUNE OF JOY. IT WAS the *sheva brachos* of Rashi's daughter Miriam. She had married a young man named Yehudah ben Nassan.

Not long afterward, Rashi's third and last daughter Rachel married a man named Eliezer.

It was late at night. The guests had gone home; everyone was asleep. In the *beis midrash* oven, a chip of wood fell into the coals, and a yellow flame leaped up. In the deserted street came the triumphant and self-abandoned, yet lonely, cry of a rooster. The stars shone without haste or judgment.

In his chambers, Rashi stirred. He had married off his three daughters to three *talmidei chachamim*, from whom he could expect the most promising future.

Not all weddings were so hopeful. One such broken marriage eventually came to the attention of Rashi.

The following is a creatively reconstructed rendering of that case.

In Rashi's private study, the hollow-eyed man gazed out the window at the clouds that fretted the pink sky, rising into a shadowy mass of cloud. He turned to Rashi and began speaking in a confidential murmur.

"When I came to visit my sister months after her marriage—for I had been away in foreign lands and could not join her earlier—I had hoped for joyous tidings. I did not know of the man she had married, except that he was of a decent family and earned his wage. He was a carpenter, she'd written me, and could also learn Torah. And so she had entertained the liveliest hopes of beginning a new and happier life after the death of our beloved parents in our youth.

"I hurried back to Troyes to visit her and her newfound family, anticipating joy, riding ever closer to the heart of what was to become an impenetrable mystery."

He fell silent a moment. The sky was turning crimson. "As I came closer, I heard reports about her husband—his name was Curt. Some told how great he was. 'He had gone to Troyes to be the best carpenter, he had a plan that would redeem the Jews from poverty . . .' Yet others hinted at unspeakable debaucheries, at fits of temper and vicious self-indulgence.

"And as I travelled ever closer to Troyes, it seemed that the figure of Curt grew until he dwarfed the surrounding landscape, and I could see nothing but him before my eyes. Still, I travelled deeper and deeper into the country, into the heart of the mystery.

"I did not get to see Curt. That is to say, at least not at first. At first, I only saw my sister—his wife.

"As I entered the town and strode upon the street where she had told me they resided, I saw a mass of Jews standing upon the street, as though upon the bank of a great river. They raised their fists and yelled at a building that stood across the way, whose fastened shutter was black, like the heart of an unfathomable secret. I could hear them shouting, 'Curt, Curt!'

"And then, from amidst that roiling crowd, there opened up a space, as though giving way to a swelling wave. A woman burst forth, her face turned away from me and to that impenetrable building, her arms raised up before her. She turned her face, and I saw that it was she, my sister. And in her eyes was an expression of unspeakable longing, suffering and hopelessness.

"She stood there in that pose a moment, an infinity—who can tell?—and then, with heart-breaking submission, let her arms fall. Her head dropped, and she stepped back into that sea of seething, angry Jews who again raised their hands, shouting, 'Curt! Curt!'

"I saw her later at my inn. She had no place of her own. In the deepening, inexpressible gloom, it seemed that the only illumination was the white smoothness of her innocent forehead.

"She told me in faltering words of the dark events that had unfolded since I had begun my journey to her and to the mysterious Curt.

"'After we first married,' she told me, 'Curt had the greatest plans. He would reform the Jews. With his carpentry, he would make the Jews into a better people, a finer people . . . He had a pamphlet written. Here!'

"She handed me a sheaf of pages, which I riffled through. Upon it, I glanced at words of noble intent and grand purpose: 'the amelioration of the race'; 'the uplifting of the national spirit'; 'for the ever-lasting glory . . .'—all written in a firm and sure handwriting. But on the last sheet, I saw at the bottom of the page, written in a degraded handwriting, spidery, hasty, 'More bitter than death!'

"'He was good to me at first,' my sister spoke to me. 'He

hoped that together we could bring a good life to the Jews of Troyes. But as I helped him in his carpentry, I grew ill. Perhaps the fumes that permeated the spectral shop affected me. Like a creeping darkness spreading into a heart of darkness, I contracted a skin disease. When Curt saw I suffered this, he thrust me out of the house and spurned me miserably. He will neither take me back nor support me!'

"In the steadily darkening room, only the fair face of my sister, standing tall in a black, deep-folded dress, seemed to shine.

"The next day, I went to see Curt. A smooth-faced Russian beggar dressed in motley danced before me in the street, and pointed out the way. 'When you see Curt, give him my regards. He is a great man! A great benefactor!'

"I followed the fantastic fool's directions and came to Curt's workshop.

"I entered the ramshackle building and encountered Curt. He was a tall, emaciated man whose bones shuffled within him. His face was topped by sparse white hair, and his skin was pulled so tight that his head seemed a skull across which flesh had been pressed taut.

"He spoke to me in a hollow, rattling voice that seemed to come from beyond the river separating death from life. 'I shall not give your sister any settlement,' he said. 'I say she had her skin disease before we married, and she didn't tell me. Had I known of it, I never would have taken her.' His large, heavy head shivered on his wrinkled neck, and he looked at me with a fantastic gleam in his black eyes. 'Now leave me!' It seemed to me that his eyes were the center of a map of mystery, the black core of a country of darkness."

The man fell silent. The flaming sky had turned vermillion, and the dark bands of cloud were black bars that held behind them an incomprehensible enigma.

Rashi replied, "This is my answer to you and your sister.

Her former husband has no argument against her whatsoever. He cannot claim that she was physically unfit before he married her.

"This man has acted in an evil manner, showing that he is not a child of Avraham Avinu, for it is the way of the Jewish people to have compassion for others.

"This holds especially true for his wife, who is his own flesh, with whom he entered into a matrimonial covenant.

"If this man had devoted himself as much to bringing her close to him as he did to casting her away, he would have made her attractive in his eyes. As our Sages said, 'A woman's grace is in her husband's eyes.' How fortunate he would have been if he had merited this woman and, through her, life in the world-to-come.

"Even among gentiles who deny G-d, we have seen many instances where they treat their wives lovingly and where the women treat their husbands lovingly.

"Yet this man hardened his heart against a Jewish woman, a daughter of our Father in Heaven.

"How terrible to break up a marriage. G-d Himself compares His relationship with the Jews as a relationship with 'the wife of His youth.'

"My judgment is that this man must treat this woman with the respect that a Jew deserves. He must either take her back into his household and treat her with compassion and honor, or divorce her and pay her the full settlement as stated in the kesubah." (*Teshuvos Chachmei Tzarfas Velothar*, 40)

11

Commentary on the Torah

IT WAS A FRIDAY AFTERNOON. RASHI SAT IN HIS GREAT STONE CHAIR, teaching a group of students the weekly *parshah*.

"In this *pasuk*," he said, "we must differentiate between the literal meaning of the verse—*mashmao shel mikra*—and its intended meaning—*peshuto shel mikra*."

One of the students, himself a *talmid chacham*, made a comment.

"Yes, Shemaya, that's an interesting *Midrash*. One can give many interpretations of this *pasuk*. The words of the Torah are like a hammer that smashes a rock and splits it into various reasons, as *Chazal* teach in *Shabbos* 88b. But my purpose is to present the simple meaning of the verse. Although there are many *Aggadic Midrashim*, what I am trying to do here is only to give the simple meaning of the verse." (*Rashi* on *Bereishis* 3:8)

90

Rashi decided to devote his time to composing a commentary on the Torah.

Tradition tells us that before Rashi began this commentary, he fasted for six hundred and thirteen days, corresponding to the number of *mitzvos* in the Torah. (*Shem Hagedolim*)

This helped Rashi gain the high spiritual level he had to reach before beginning his work. As the Chida wrote, "Apparently, Rashi wrote his commentary by using a secret [technique to gain G-dly inspiration], and therefore he fasted six hundred and thirteen times." (*Shem Hagedolim*)

The Chida states that although Rashi's commentary seems to be dealing with the simple meaning of the text, "his words contain supernal hints."

Rabbi Mordechai Yaffe wrote similarly that "all the words of Rashi have a revealed and hidden part—and both are true." (*Levush Haoraah* on *Bereishis*)

(There is also a story told in *yeshivos* that a Kabbalist once composed a commentary on the *Chumash*. After being told successive times by his teacher to shorten and simplify his commentary, he realized that he now had an exact copy of Rashi's commentary; and so he gave up his endeavor.)

Rashi opened his commentary with a *Midrash*: "Rabbi Yitzchak said . . ." Some say that he did so in order to allude to his father's name at the very beginning of his work.

"According to an old manuscript from the land of Israel," the Taz wrote in his work on Rashi's commentary called *Divrei Dovid*, "Rashi's father was not very learned. This is not true, though, for we find that Rashi quotes his father by name at the end of *Avodah Zarah*. At any rate, Rashi wished to honor his father by mentioning him at the beginning of his work."

Peirush Rashi Al Hatorah has become the most common commentary on the Torah; the first commentary studied by schoolchildren.

It is the lens through which Jews see the *Chumash*.

Like Rashi's commentary on the Talmud, his commentary on the Torah was clear and well-rounded. But in addition, his commentary seems more than the creation of human intellect alone. In this work, Rashi was seemingly divinely inspired to choose out of the enormous quantity of material that he knew the precisely correct comment to make that would reflect the truth of Torah and illumine the mind of the student. Thus, his commentary became a work of unparalleled greatness. The commentaries of the greatest *Rishonim* could not displace Rashi—to the contrary, they are often concerned with discussing his comments.

In the most masterful fashion possible, Rashi blended together *Midrashim*, comments on grammar, and clarification of the words in all aspects: clarifying a story, a *halachah*, or explaining how something in the Mishkan was constructed.

Rashi's commentary contains his wise, loving and peaceable spirit. Often, he would use the occasion of a phrase in the *Chumash* to cite a *Midrash* that stresses the importance of goodness and love.

Rashi's commentary on the Torah breathes an atmosphere of purity and goodness. Like the words of the Torah itself, his commentary can be studied at every age to yield new wisdom.

The Jewish people have treated Rashi's commentary on the Torah with a mixture of awe and homeyness. He is the great teacher; yet he is also one's companion since childhood. Even as an adult, one feels as though one is being held by the hand and led through each phrase of the *Chumash* by a wise and self-effacing teacher.

Rashi's commentary on the Torah is more than wise; in a sense, more than true. It is Torah itself. When one learns the commentary, one is affected by its spirit of humility, piety, simplicity and desire for truth. It is a living document, for it lives within everyone who learns it.

In Rashi's day, there were two major schools of studying the *Chumash*. One was the school of *derash*, based on the *Midrashim* and *aggadeta* of *Chazal*. The other school was that of the *masorah* and *peshat*, dedicated to attaining a basic understanding of the structure of the text and the simple meaning of the words. (These schools were, of course, not mutually exclusive. One could not learn *derash* unless one knew the simple meaning of the words, and one could not provide a translation of numerous phrases without reference to the interpretations of *Chazal*.)

Rashi's commentary was a blending of these two schools. Rashi's commentary blended *peshat* with *derash* that was close to *peshat*.

The Friday afternoon *shiur* on the Torah continued.

A student raised his hand. "The *rosh yeshivah* has seemingly dismissed the explanation of the *Midrash*. But how can this be? These are the explanations of *Chazal*!"

"That is true," Rashi replied. "But one must ask what the purpose of a comment is. Our rabbis have presented *derashos*. But my purpose is to explain the *pesukim* in context and in their order." (Rashi on *Shemos* 33:13)

Another student raised his hand. He was a mature man who was writing commentaries on *Nach* (although unavailable for centuries, they were recently published).

"Yes, Reb Yosef?"

"*Rebbi*, when I learned with my uncle, Rabbi Menachem ben Chelbo, *zichrono livrachah*, he taught that . . ."

Another student whispered to himself, "Yes, I saw that in his *Pisronim*!"

Rabbi Menachem's *Pisronim*—Explanations—was the first known Ashkenazi commentary on *Tanach*. This commentary stressed *peshat*. (Only fragments of this work still exist.)

"That is a fascinating statement," Rashi said after Rabbi Yosef finished. "I will take note of it in my own commentary on the *Chumash*."

Rashi's commentaries on the Torah and on *Nach* apparently grew out of the *shiurim* he gave to his students. Rashi's students, *talmidei chachamim* in their own right, studied what he taught them and then, either in *shiur* or privately, discussed points with him. (Lipschitz) In his great modesty, Rashi took his students' comments seriously, and they enriched and informed his commentary. Thus did this great work slowly form. Only toward the last years of Rashi's life was it at last completed.

In writing his commentary on the Torah, Rashi made great use of *Midrash*. He had access to many *Midrashic* works, including some collections that had been put together only recently. Some of his editions were more complete than the works we possess today. He also was familiar with works that are not extant today; sometimes he quoted *Midrashim* that are no longer in existence.

One of the most famous *darshanim* was Rabbi Moshe Hadarshan, apparently from the generation preceding that of Rashi. Rashi cited him often.

Rashi's primary interest, he wrote, was to give the *peshat* of the *pesukim*. When he used *Midrash*, he did so with this purpose in mind.

"There are an endless number of *Aggadic Midrashim*," Rashi wrote on *Bereishis* 6:3, "but [my explanation] is the clear, simple answer." At times, it was obvious to Rashi that the plain meaning of the verse could only be understood in the light of a *Midrash*. On the very first *pasuk* of the Torah, Rashi exclaimed, "This verse cries out, 'Interpret me in accordance with our rabbis' interpretation.'"

As a result of Rashi's work, many tales, interpretations and homilies of the *Midrash* and *Gemara* that had been scattered in voluminous and hard-to-get manuscripts became the accessible heritage of the Jewish people.

Rashi's commitment to the truth was extraordinary. If he did not feel completely sure that he understood a *pasuk* correctly, he would humbly write: "I do not know what this comes to teach us" (*Bereishis* 28:5); "I do not know what the word 'dim'a' means" (*Shemos* 22:28). There is no doubt that Rashi could have speculated brilliantly about the meaning of these *pesukim*. There is no question that he knew the meaning of the *pesukim* as clearly as others who do explain them. But Rashi demanded of himself a higher level of certainty; a higher level of truth. When he felt that he had not attained that, he did not attempt to speculate.

According to tradition, Rashi had had difficulty trying to understand what the *ephod* looked like. One day he happened to raise his eyes at the precise moment that a woman on horseback rode by. Normally, Rashi walked with his eyes cast to the ground, looking no further ahead of him than four *amos*. Now he was anguished. What was the reason that he had, however inadvertently, interrupted his pious behavior and looked upon a woman? Was there something wrong with his service of G-d? Immediately, he realized that the woman's apron resembled the *ephod*. This episode had been brought about by Heaven so that he would understand and be able to explain the *Chumash* better. In his commentary, he wrote, "The *ephod* is made like the apron that women wear when riding on a horse." (Rashi on *Shemos* 28:7)

Rashi's grandson, the great *Baal Tosefos*, Rabbeinu Tam, later wrote, "I could have duplicated my grandfather's commentary on the *Gemara*; but I could not duplicate his commentary on the *Chumash*." (*Shem Hagedolim*)

In the fourteenth century, a commentator named Rabbi Zalman (descendant of Rabbeinu Meshullam Hagadol) pointed out that the first letter in Rashi's commentary is an *alef*—the first letter of the alphabet; and the last letter is a *tav*—the last letter of the alphabet. Rashi's commentary is all-inclusive.

Almost as soon as it was written, Rashi's commentary was accepted by all Jewish communities, Ashkenazi and Sephardi, as authoritative. It speaks to all students, of all ages and all levels of sophistication. The universality of Rashi's commentary is reflected in the *halachah* that one can fulfill one's responsibility of reading the *Targum* of the weekly *parshah* by learning Rashi on the *parshah*.

Because Rashi is the first commentary that a child learns, there is the danger that one may mistake Rashi as being simple or basic. But in the commentary of Rashi, one might say, the Torah speaks through Rashi's pen. With his profound ability to distill the most profound concepts into pithy sayings, Rashi presented the depths of Torah in a fashion that all Jews could relate to. Just as the small space of the *Mishkan* courtyard was able to hold all the Jews (Rashi on *Vayikra* 8:3), so are all Jews able to stand within the boundaries of the Torah by studying the holy words of Rashi on the Torah.

12

Rashi's Odyssey

ACCORDING TO TRADITION, RASHI LEFT HIS NATIVE TROYES AND returned to Worms, where he became *rosh yeshivah.* (*Shem Hagedolim*)

The *beis midrash* where Rashi is said to have learned stood until *Teves*, 1939, when it was destroyed by the Nazis.

The synagogue was a house with a steep, tiled roof. Inside, elaborate candle chandeliers hung from the high roof, and light streamed in from large, lozenge-like windows in the thick walls.

Abutting this synagogue on the right was the domed chapel, a long room where Rashi was said to study with his students. In the middle of the room was a stone table, next to which stood a chair of stone, where Rashi was supposed to have sat when teaching. In the wall opposite the chapel, the letter *alef* was carved. Once, it is said, when Rashi found his

97

students unprepared, he pointed at the *alef*, hinting that they should consider themselves beginners.

Years back, it had been in the very alley adjacent to this chapel that Rashi's mother had pressed against the wall that had miraculously sunken in to save her life and that of her unborn baby. Now Rashi had returned here as if to vindicate that miracle and teach Torah.

Other stories tell of Rashi going to Narbonne, in Provence, to learn in the *yeshivah* of Rabbi Moshe Hadarshan. Some even tell that Rashi went to learn in the *yeshivah* of Rabbi Zerachiah Halevi, the Razah, in Lunel (also in Provence). This cannot be true, because the Razah was born twenty years after Rashi passed away.

For eight years, tradition holds, Rashi worked on his commentaries on the *Gemara* and *Chumash*, not showing them to others. Then, when he was thirty-three years old, he decided to go into exile and anonymously disseminate his *kuntresim*.

On the basis of this tradition, many tales were told over hundreds of years about Rashi's travels and adventures, and about how the acclaim that his commentaries met forced him to reveal himself.

To what degree these stories are true is impossible to say. Together they form a colorful, exotic odyssey in the popular history of the great teacher of Israel.

Rashi stood at the window of the *beis midrash*, gazing out in abstracted thought. There was a rustle behind him, and Rashi turned about. His trusted student Shemaya stood at the doorway.

"*Rebbi*, a letter has come from a far-flung Jewish community. They desire that you send them a copy of your *kuntresim* on the *Gemara*."

"I am afraid that I cannot do that."

"But, *Rebbi*, why not?"

Rashi turned up his palms. "Who is to say that I am worthy?"

"You, *Rebbi*, doubt that you are worthy?"

"Yes, I do, Shemaya. Who am I to say that my commentary is better than—or, for that matter, as good as—anything being taught in other *batei midrash*? Somewhere, there may be a *talmid chacham* whose work is superior to mine. It is his *kuntresim* that should be publicized."

"But, *Rebbi*," Shemaya protested, "how could you ever be sure of this without travelling through the entire world, visiting hundreds of Jewish communities?"

"Ah! You are right, Shemaya. That is the only way that I could truly be sure."

Rashi gazed out the window in thought. Shemaya backed out of the room and soundlessly shut the door.

Indeed—that was what he would do: travel throughout the world and visit *batei midrash* anonymously. In every *beis midrash*, he would distribute some of his *kuntresim* and see what sort of reception they received. He would sit in a thousand *Gemara shiurim* and learn whether any other *talmid chacham* deserved to have his *kuntresim* publicized.

How long would this take? Two years? Seven? It did not matter. What mattered was the honor of the Torah.

In the street, a group of girls walked by. The sound of their voices drifted up to him, young and happy. They were dressed modestly, radiating innocence. Would he leave this?

Out on the road, he would pass through degraded scenes bare of any tinge of Torah. He would pass inns where young men and women sat at small tables, the men wearing earrings and ponytails, while in the street, sleek men rode by upon their horses, gaining their evening exercise. He would leave the sanctity of the *beis midrash* and spend his time travelling among people who never thought of G-d and Torah.

Yet the conviction grew upon Rashi that he must go into a self-imposed exile. As a child, he had grown up in the midst of Torah, filled with the joy of the Torah's holiness. The yearning of his heart to do G-d's will and to know G-d's intent had been fulfilled as he sat among other *talmidei chachamim* studying the word of G-d through the words of the holy *Tanaim* and *Amoraim*.

Yet there had always been a sorrow, a bitter inbite of conscience that gnawed at his heart, a corroding guilt. He knew that his father had cast away a precious jewel in return for which deed he had been rewarded with a son. Rashi realized that although his father had been delighted to give up the jewel for the sake of Heaven, there had still been a small part of him that had grieved to lose the treasure that could have made him fabulously wealthy.

Rashi felt guilty for having been connected to this secret grief of his father.

Perhaps, he considered, by going into a self-imposed exile, he would expiate that grief.

The next day, Rashi started planning his itinerary. He sat in his study, a map spread across the table. First he would head down to Spain—he would be able to stop in Narbonne on the way. From Spain, he would sail over to Italy, where he could visit the holy community in Rome. From there, he would visit the communities of Greece and then sail for Egypt. From Egypt, he could take a caravan up to Eretz Yisrael. After Eretz Yisrael—Babylonia! And from Babylonia, he would return to Europe, but this time, after he arrived at Bordeaux, he would head way up north through Mainz to Prague. Then he would turn about and go back home.

The next morning, Rashi took tearful leave of his wife, his daughters, his sons-in-law and his beloved students. A knapsack on his back and a walking staff in hand, he set out on his laborious journey.

As he continued his itinerary, visiting towns and cities, he would secretly slip copies of his *kuntresim* into a copy of the *Gemara*. He would then sit in the back of the *beis midrash* and see how people reacted.

Invariably, the *talmid chacham* who found the *kuntres* would be delighted. His eyes would light up in joy as he read Rashi's holy words. "Who slipped this into my *Gemara?*" he would question all the rabbis in the community. But no one would suspect the modest stranger who sat in the rear of the *beis midrash*.

So valued were these *kuntresim* that people began copying them and spreading them abroad. They became famous as *Peirush Hakuntres*.

And so, day after weary day, did Rashi travel: out of Champagne to Orleans, southward through Berry, Bourbonnais, Marche, Limousin, and ever southward, to Guyenne, Gascony, and Toulouse.

As the days turned into weeks and months, Rashi's clothes grew ragged. Often he did not have enough to eat. He would come into a town famished, his shoes ragged. His first question would always be: "Where is the *beis midrash?*" Amidst the hundreds of wandering mendicants, no one suspected that this might be more than another homeless beggar.

In one town, a banquet was being held in honor of a circumcision.

When Rashi stepped into the *beis midrash*, a heavy man stepped up to him.

"My name is André. You can sit over there." He pointed to the end of the table, where the beggars and were sitting.

The room was filled with the murmur of conversation and the sound of cutlery clinking on china. Rashi made his way down alongside the table, where men in their *Yom Tov* suits were bent over their plates. The scent of spiced meat wafted up to Rashi. He had not had a satisfying meal in days. Finally,

he came to the end of the table. There he squeezed onto a
bench next to a dirty mendicant with a sallow face and a short,
bristling moustache.

"Down with the rich!" the mendicant exclaimed. He
waved his fork at the company before them. "Look how much
they have—and how they treat us, throwing us bones!" He
gestured to his plate, upon which lay a tough leg of chicken.

Rashi sat silently at his place.

A waiter passed down the long table, handing out plates
of dressed veal and bouillabaisse to the chattering guests. Just
before he came to Rashi, he returned to the kitchen.

A few minutes later, he came back and placed before Rashi
a plate containing a thin, gamy cockerel—the cheapest and
most unappetizing piece of meat.

What a slap in the face!

"You see? I was right!" the man sitting next to Rashi said.
"The wealthy stuff their faces with their ill-gotten gains and
feed us the crumbs off their groaning tables to keep us from
rising up against them!"

Rashi did not respond to the hot-headed young man. But
picking up the dry, tough leg of the cockerel, he broke out in
a loud song, "When we were low, He remembered us, for His
lovingkindness is forever!" (*Tehillim* 136:23)

At the head of the table, there was an indignant commotion.

But Rashi kept singing the verse again and again. "When
we were low, He remembered us, for His lovingkindness is
forever!"

A number of leading *talmidei chachamim* were sitting at
the dais. They walked over to Rashi.

"Sir," one of them asked, "why are you disturbing the joy
of the banquet?"

Rashi said nothing in return, but held his plate out before
them.

One of the *talmidei chachamim* picked up the piece of meat and inspected it. "I get it!" he said. "This is a cockerel. This man keeps singing 'When we were low, He remembered—*zachar*—us,' which can also be understood as, 'When we were low, we were given a male—*zachor*—chicken!'"

Another *talmid chacham* said, "And the end of the *pasuk*: 'for His lovingkindness is forever!' In other words, even though this man has been given this poor food, he still has faith in G-d's goodness and rejects the vain pleasures of this world."

Rashi smiled. They had understood him.

"Our deepest apologies!" the first *talmid chacham* said. "You are obviously a man of wisdom. Come up to the head and address us."

All of the rabbis pressed Rashi to speak, until he acquiesced. As he rose from his place, the man next to him muttered darkly, "So you're turning your back on the poor working folk, are you?"

"You are a very contentious young man," Rashi replied. "But controversy is hateful, and peace is wonderful. Set your heart to pursue peace, for if peace is lacking, then there is nothing." (*Teshuvah*)

At the head of the table, Rashi talked with such inspiration that it seemed that his words were coming directly from Har Sinai.

The scholars at the head of the table as one thought of the *pasuk*, "Honor her [wisdom], and she will lift you." (*Mishlei* 4:8)—that is, she will place you among princes. (*Hagados Ketuos*)

Rashi continued his travels, preceded by his anonymous *kuntresim*.

One day, as he sat in a *beis midrash*, he heard a *rosh yeshivah* teaching the *Gemara* with his commentary. From time to time, one student would say to the other in frustration,

"This line of the *kuntres* is hard to understand."

Rashi walked over to them. "Maybe I can help you. I believe that these statements can be explained in the following way."

As he proceeded to speak, everyone was amazed that this simple beggar so brilliantly explained the *kuntres*.

Finally, it became clear that he was actually the author of the *kuntresim*.

"Please teach us!" the *rosh yeshivah* asked him.

"Very well," Rashi said. "For as long as I remain in your city. But only on condition that you tell no one else. In this way, I will teach Torah not only in writing, but orally as well. Thus, I shall fulfill the *pasuk*, 'Write yourselves this song; teach it to the children of Israel; place it in their mouths.'" (Rashi in Yiddish, Yehudah Halevi Dassauer).

A similar story was told in *chassidic* circles.

The people of a certain town realized that the ignorant pauper who had come to their *beis midrash* might be the great *rosh yeshivah* of Troyes. "Come, let us look after him and learn from his actions!"

But by the time they came to the *beis midrash*, Rashi had already left the town.

A messenger on horseback rushed down to the road and overtook Rashi. Coming into the next town, he told the rabbis that a man who might be the great Rashi of Troyes was on his way.

"Many beggars pass through our town," someone objected, "and we have no famous *beis midrash*. Maybe he will slip through our fingers."

"I have an idea!" said the messenger. "I will make a meal here for all the poor people. This man, who is wandering about with no money, will surely come. Then we will be able to examine his actions and see if he is really Rashi."

The feast was arranged. When Rashi came into the room,

the messenger recognized him. "Here, sir!" He took Rashi by the arm. "We have prepared a place for you at the head of the table."

"Me? At the head of the table? What do you want from me?"

The rabbis looked at each other. Was this Rashi—or a simple person?

They decided to put him to another test.

At the end of the meal, a cup was brought before him. "We are honoring you to lead the *Birkas Hamazon*."

One of the rabbis poured wine into the cup.

"Don't fill the cup to the top!" Rashi commanded.

The rabbis looked at each other. Now they might hear a *halachic* insight.

"Why not?"

"Because my jacket is almost new, and I don't want wine to spill on it."

The rabbis looked at each other in disappointment. If this was the famous Rashi, he was concealing himself too well.

This story was told to Rabbi Menachem Mendel, the Kotzker Rebbe. He said, "This was in truth Rashi." These words of his hinted at Kabbalistic mysteries. (*Mifalos Tzaddikim*)

Rashi continued on his travels, southward into Spain: Pamplona, Sangüesa, Calahorra . . . The winter rains had begun to fall. The roads were muddy, and the wind blew through his mantle.

At last he reached Tudela.

He walked along a winding street and came to an inn. A ragged pennant blew in the rainy wind, an illustration of a wine barrel on a yellow background. Rashi opened the door. There was a waft of warm air with the scent of coal and spices. A guitar gave a flourish. A man was dancing, clicking his heels against the wooden floor. Opposite him, flouncing in yellow and black skirts, a woman raised her arms and beat a staccato on castanets.

Rashi let the door close. The music, the warmth, the spicy smell of food disappeared. He was alone again and hungry in the cold drizzle.

He walked on in the rain. Drenched, he didn't try to protect himself from the cold drops that beat against his face.

"Hey, you!"

Rashi looked up. He had wandered onto a wealthy street. A butler was shaking the debris out of a basket. "Get a move on!"

"Do you know where I can find the *beis midrash*?" Rashi asked. He would rather sleep on a bench than in the inn with the guitar player and the flashing dancer.

"The other way, half a mile." The butler withdrew into the house and shut the door.

Rashi sighed and turned around.

The streets turned and twisted, and soon Rashi was lost, walking up the broad stairs of an alley between vine-hung walls.

At the top of the hill, there was a black, wrought-iron gate. Noting the large *mezuzah* on the gate, Rashi turned onto the walk.

A black-eyed servant answered the door. "Come in, please! You look soaked."

"Thank you."

"One moment. I'll get a towel. Take off your shoes, and I'll bring some slippers."

Soon Rashi was sitting in a chair, a blanket wrapped about him, drinking from a steaming cup.

"You are very kind."

"My master has told me always to welcome guests."

"What is his name?"

"Rabbi Yehudah Halevi."

"How extraordinary!" Rashi said. "That is exactly the man I came to Tudela to see! Could you please inform him that Shlomo Yitzchaki of Troyes is here?"

"I am afraid he isn't in. He should be back this evening."

An hour later, Rashi excused himself to go to the *bets midrash*.

As he was walking down the narrow street, he heard footsteps behind him. He turned around—it was the black-eyed servant. The rain had pasted one of his *peyos* across his cheek like a dash of paint, and he looked angry.

"What is it—?"

The servant grabbed Rashi's arm. "Come with me."

"Yes, but—"

The servant pulled Rashi along gruffly.

When they returned, another servant was standing in the vestibule.

"Give us the silk robe!"

"I don't know what you gentlemen—"

"Come on! There was a silk robe here on the hook, and when you left, it was gone."

"I'm sorry, I—"

The second servant took hold of Rashi's knapsack and pawed through it. "It isn't here."

"Take off your coat."

Humiliated, Rashi let the servants look under his coat.

The second servant lifted Rashi's purse from his belt. "If you don't have the robe with you, you can at least pay for it." He spilled the coins into his hand and counted them out. "That should cover it, more or less."

The first servant handed Rashi back his purse, coat and knapsack. "You can go. We aren't thieves."

A minute later, the heavy, mahogany door slammed shut behind Rashi. He stood again in the slanting rain. He took a chalky rock from the ground and wrote in large Hebrew letters on the front door: Shlomo Shlomo Shlomo Shlomo Shlomo.

In the early evening, when Rabbi Yehudah Halevi returned home, he saw the white Hebrew letters, broken up by the steady drizzle but still legible.

When he came into the house, the first servant came up to take his coat. "Moshe, what is that writing on the door?"

"Writing . . . ?" The servant looked at the door. "There was a man who came to see you today. He said he was a Rabbi Shlomo from Troyes. After he left . . ." The servant told everything that had happened. "But I don't know why he wrote that."

"You fool!" Rabbi Yehudah Halevi exclaimed. "Don't you know that I put away that silken robe this afternoon?"

"Then—then he didn't take the robe?"

"No," Rabbi Yehudah Halevi said. "You have deeply insulted a *talmid chacham*."

"Rabbi, a thousand pardons."

"Go and find Rabbi Shlomo immediately and bring him back to me!"

"At once, sire!"

The servant ran into the street, sick with remorse. Rabbi Shlomo wasn't in the inn—no one had seen him there. Moshe went to the *beis midrash*—and there he found Rabbi Shlomo. What was he doing? He seemed to be slipping some pages into a *Gemara*. But that didn't matter now.

The servant rushed up before Rashi and bowed his head.

"Rabbi Shlomo, a thousand pardons! Please accept my tear-stained apology! My master, Rabbi Yehudah Halevi is home. He wishes that you dine with him."

Placating the servant, Rashi picked up his knapsack and followed him back.

Back in the house, Rabbi Yehudah Halevi stood before a fire. "My deepest apologies, my friend. My servants, I fear,

were over-zealous. I have rebuked them for their malfea-
sance. Let me get you a change of clothing and a hot tea."

Soon the two great *talmidei chachamim* were sitting
before the fire. The heat soaked through Rashi's bones, and he
sighed in pleasure.

As Rabbi Yehudah Halevi spoke with Rashi, he realized
that Rashi was a wise and deeply-learned person.

"There is one thing I don't understand," Rabbi Yehudah
Halevi said. "Why did you write that cryptic message on my
door: 'Shlomo Shlomo Shlomo Shlomo Shlomo'?"

"It was a message to you, the wisest of all men," Rashi said.
"But if you wish, I shall decipher it. One must merely change
the vowel marks so that the words read: *Shelama Shlomo
salmah shleimah shilmah*? 'Why did Shlomo have to pay for
an entire garment?'"

Rabbi Yehudah Halevi burst into a hearty laugh, and he
raised his glass. "*Lechaim!*" (R' Maimon)

During his stay in Tudela, Rashi met with many great
rabbis and wealthy people. Once, he stayed with the *parnas*,
or civil ruler, of the Jews of Castille, who did a great deal of
good for the Jews. There is a tradition that at his request, Rashi
wrote a *sefer* and named it for him: "*Sefer Haparnes.*"
(*Shalsheles Hakabbalah*) It was Rashi's intent in doing so to
honor people who do good deeds. (*Kav Hayashar*) (Actually,
Rashi is the inspiration and main source for *Sefer Hapardes*.
There is a *Sefer Haparnes*—but it was written two hundred
years later by Rabbi Moshe Parnes, a student of the Maharam
of Rothenberg.)

Then Rashi was on his way again. He travelled eastward
across the breadth of Castille and into Aragon, reaching the
port city of Barcelona. From there he sailed in a barque across
the Mediterranean Sea, passing through the Strait of Bonifacio,
separating the islands of Corsica and Sardinia. There he passed
the merry, brown-faced fishermen of the isles, leaning out

precariously from their vessels.

Rashi's ship set to port at Anzio. From there, he travelled inland and to the north, until he came to Rome, and entered the *beis midrash* where Rabbi Moshe Hadarshan had taught.

Now Rashi travelled southward, past Velletri, where wandering minstrels displayed dancing bears. Along the Liri River, he went down past Capua, then Caserta, Benevento, Aversa and, finally, Naples.

Here a sturdy merchant ship took him down to the community of Palermo, on the large island of Sicily. From there he travelled by donkey with a group of merchants to the Jewish community of Messina. Then, on another merchant ship, he travelled down the Strait of Messina around the toe of the boot of Italy, continuing due east.

Passing the Ionian Sea to the north, the ship sailed to the island of Crete, where the Grecian Jews lived. And then they sailed on again through the Sea of Crete, where the hundred islands of Greece were scattered like burning jewels upon a sparkling, turquoise sea.

On the island of Rhodes, just south of Turkey, Rashi met with the members of the ancient Jewish community.

Then his ship made the long journey cutting southeast across the breadth of the Mediterranean, and finally, after a week of sailing, came to port in Alexandria, Egypt, in the north of Africa. Rashi hired a donkey from his meager funds, and travelled southward along a tributary of the Nile, its waters swollen and muddy, rolling northward.

At last, Rashi came to Cairo.

Here, tradition says (based on the testimony of the Jews of Salonica), Rashi met with Rabbi Moshe ben Maimon—the Rambam. According to this tradition, Rashi stayed in Rabbi Moshe ben Maimon's house. The Rambam was greatly impressed by Rashi's wisdom, and made him a gift of balsam oil, a precious ointment worth its weight in gold. The two men stayed together for many days.

In addition, Rashi showed some of his *kuntresim* to the Rambam. So impressed was the Rambam that he wrote a letter telling that although he himself had considered writing such a commentary on the *Gemara*, now he saw that there was no longer a need for it, since "the Frenchman," as he called Rashi, had already done so. (*Shalsheles Hakabbalah*)

However, this folk tradition cannot be true, for the Rambam was born twenty years after Rashi passed away.

Now Rashi travelled northward, to Eretz Yisrael.

From Eretz Yisrael, he again travelled due east, plodding inland, through desert and primitive Arab villages, where the dogs howled every night and the women were dark, fleeting shadows dressed in long black robes that only allowed their eyes to show.

Finally, he came to Persia, where he visited the glorious *yeshivos* that had been the citadels of the *Geonim*.

There, in the fabulous lands of the East, Rashi met a learned priest who was also travelling across the globe on a religious pilgrimage.

This priest was fascinated by the Torah. He engaged Rashi in long philosophical discussions and was stirred by Rashi's wisdom.

Late at night, the two men could be seen strolling back and forth along the sandy city streets. Sometimes, they would walk out into the desert, where passing caravansaries, led by haughty camels, plodded by, laden with spices and grain.

One day, the priest fell ill.

Rashi knew a good deal about medicine and tended to the priest. He prepared poultices and healing teas. The disease had been caused by the noxious blowfly, and Rashi, knowing of the remedy for the dread lassitude and fever that would fall upon a man in consequence, cared for the priest with a steady dedication, remaining at his bedside day and night with a damp towel in his hand to wipe the priest's fevered brow.

At long last, after weeks of uncertainty, the priest came back from the brink of death and slowly, though sallow and frail, regained his health.

One day, as the priest was sitting up in bed, Rashi entered his room.

The priest looked up. "My friend! You are wearing your knapsack and carrying your walking staff. Can this mean . . . ?"

"Yes. Now that I am assured that you have recovered, I shall again set out upon my lengthy journey."

The priest reached down under his mattress. "Here. Take these precious jewels. They are worth a fortune."

"No, I—"

"I want you to have them."

"But I cannot—"

"I insist!"

"I cannot take a gift from you," Rashi said. "You owe me nothing. Although you and I are of different faiths, we are both human beings, created in the image of G-d. My Torah obligates me to help all people in need."

"But you must allow me to show my gratitude. To do otherwise would be cruel!"

"If that is so," Rashi said, "this is what I ask. If ever you meet a Jew who is in trouble, help him with the same faithfulness that I attended to you during your illness."

"I give you my hand upon that."

Rashi took the priest's outstretched hand. For long moments, they gazed into each other's eyes.

"Farewell!" Rashi said at last, unclasping his hand and turning toward the door.

"G-dspeed!" the priest replied. (*Maimon*)

Rashi retraced the steps of his long journey. But now, instead of giving out copies of his commentary on the *Gemara*, he distributed his Commentary on the Torah.

Again, he passed through Eretz Yisrael, Egypt, Rhodes, Greece, sailed back to Sicily, up to Naples and Rome, then across the sea again to Barcelona, westward to Tudela and now northward to Provence and France, coming close to his beloved home.

One day, Rashi's identity was revealed.

He had been staying in a town for a few weeks, working on his Commentary on the Torah. Doubts had assailed his mind. Was this the right thing to do? Was he the right person to do it?

One day, he heard a *bas kol*—a voice from Heaven—announcing: "A *kuntres* has fallen from Heaven!"

Rashi had received his answer. He returned to his composition with renewed energy.

The townspeople were puzzled and delighted to receive the mysterious commentaries on the *Chumash*, which kept appearing piecemeal.

One young man, a student in the *beis midrash*, conceived the idea that they were being penned and distributed by the deceptively simple-looking stranger who had only recently come into town. The student decided to keep a close eye on him.

Meanwhile, Rashi attended the *Gemara shiur* in the *beis midrash*.

One day, the rabbi couldn't understand a problem. "I have explained as much as Hashem has allowed me to understand," he said. "Any better explanation will have to wait for Eliyahu Hanavi."

Rashi, sitting in the back of the *beis midrash*, thought, I am not Eliyahu Hanavi. But in my *kuntres* on the *Gemara*, I have explained this question clearly.

Late at night, when the *beis midrash* was deserted, Rashi slipped a copy of his *kuntres* into the *Gemara*.

The next day, the rabbi and his students were astounded

at the simplicity and brilliance that Rashi's comments shed on the *Gemara.*

Suspiciously, the young student squinted at Rashi, who sat at the end of the room, apparently oblivious to the commotion.

The student continued to follow Rashi tenaciously.

Friday came. Everyone was getting ready for *Shabbos,* and the *beis midrash* was empty. Looking about to see that he was unobserved, Rashi slipped a part of his Commentary on the Torah into the *Chumash.*

A pair of eyes peered at him from the women's section. They blinked in surprise and then gleamed in triumph.

A moment later, the student slipped out the side door of the *beis midrash* and ran to the house of the town rabbi.

"Rabbi! I have discovered the identity of the mysterious stranger!"

The chief rabbi twisted his pointy beard. "Harrumph! This calls for a rabbinical synod!" His bright eyes gleamed. "We shall discuss how best to honor him."

On *Shabbos* morning, Rashi took his usual place in the back of the synagogue. The *gabbai,* a thin man with pale eyes, came up to Rashi. "We have arranged a better seat for you."

Rashi allowed the *gabbai* to lead him up to the front of the synagogue, next to the *aron kodesh* and the chief rabbi.

Then, at the reading of the Torah, Rashi was given an *aliyah,* and he was called up with the title, *Moreinu Verabbeinu*—our teacher and rabbi.

Rashi didn't know why he was being honored this way. He didn't suspect that his secret had been revealed.

The next day, when Rashi arrived at the *Gemara shiur,* all the *talmidei chachamim* were present. As soon as he stepped into the *beis midrash,* they rose and proclaimed, "Welcome, our teacher and rabbi!"

Rashi turned around, and with great feeling, he also called

out, "Welcome, our teacher and rabbi!"

"What are you doing?" the chief rabbi exclaimed.

"I am doing what you are doing," Rashi said. "You are honoring some great *talmid chacham*, so I wish to honor him as well."

"Rabbi, it is you whom we honor," the chief rabbi said. "You are the author of these wonderful *kuntresim*. We honor you now, and ask you to forgive us for not having done so before."

Looking at the chief rabbi and the *talmidei chachamim* who stood behind him, Rashi realized that he could no longer remain anonymous. He stood in silence long moments, as he realized the ramifications of that change.

"The voice of the people is like the voice of G-d," he finally said. "I see now that it has been agreed to in Heaven that my *kuntresim* be spread abroad, among all the children of Israel.

"But I have one request. I ask that you name these *kuntresim* Shai, an acronym of my name and that of my father: Shlomo Yitzchaki."

"Our teacher," the chief rabbi said. "We will do as you request. But allow us to add the letter *reish*, for Rabbi. Allow us to call your *kuntresim* by the name, Rashi." (*Heichal Rashi* and other sources)

Again, Rashi set out on his travels. Now, in whichever town he came to, people were studying the commentaries that they were already calling Rashi.

One winter night, Rashi, hungry and frozen, entered a small country inn. Outside, the wind blew miserably. Hard, icy snow covered the ground and hung upon the roof and walls of the inn. As Rashi stepped through the door, an icicle fell from the roof and smashed on the frozen ground.

In the inn, Rashi shivered and stamped his feet.

The innkeeper, a small, red-faced man with a harassed look, glanced him up and down. The look in his eye said,

"Here's a customer without money," and he didn't move from his place.

Rashi moved over to the huge stove at the end of the room and let the heat of the fire sift through him deliciously and warm his frozen body.

From the next room, he heard someone teaching *Chumash*—and then quoting from his commentary.

For long minutes, as he spread his arms out to the fire, he listened to the teacher.

How he wished he could have something to eat! But he had only a few coins left.

From the other room, he heard the teacher struggling over his words. The teacher let out a groan. "What does Rashi want?"

Rashi couldn't restrain himself. He called out, "Rashi wants a bowl of soup!" (*Maaselach un Falksverter Fun Deitshe Yidden, Morgen Zhournal*)

Now, instead of going directly home, Rashi swung to the northeast. He travelled up from Toulouse through France, up to Vienna, and then north, ever northward, stopping in Metz, Trier and Mainz, where he had learned as a student.

He continued, still bearing northwest, past Magdeburg, crossing the broad Elbe River. Finally, he entered the Kingdom of Poland, past Posen and Gnesena, until he reached, at last, the city of Prague.

Rashi's commentaries had spread across the world and won him fame. He was acclaimed as *Parshandasa*—the master of the simple explanation.

As Rashi entered the walls of Prague, a throng of Jews greeted him, accompanying him through the streets and market squares to the house of the chief rabbi.

From a narrow, leaded window, a man with a thick moustache and pomaded hair gazed down darkly.

"Patros!"

The little minister at the other end of the room leaped forward like a sparrow. "Yes, Duke Vratislav."

"Who is that rabbi that the Jews are welcoming with such celebration?"

"I—I do not know, your excellency."

"I do not like to see these Jews happy. It grates on my nerves. Patros, arrest the Jew and have him brought to me in chains."

"At once, your excellency."

Patros slipped out backwards through the double doors, smiling and nodding at Duke Vratislav.

Half an hour later, five gendarmes in red uniforms, sabers flashing at their sides, marched into the Jewish quarter.

They burst into the chief rabbi's house and placed manacles upon the wrists of Rashi.

As the gendarmes marched Rashi through the Christian section of town, faces leered through windows, from storefronts, along the streets.

Rashi, his hands chained before him, was brought into the palace.

He was left alone in a magnificent room with gilded wood paneling, until he called out, "Sentry, are you there? Just ease these darbies at the wrist!"

A pair of double doors opened. In came Duke Vratislav, dapper in a white cutaway coat and bright blue breeches. With him entered a tall, stooped bishop in flowing, purple robes, a brilliant, white plate upon his chest. Beneath his miter, his hair was shot with gray.

The duke strode up to Rashi. "So, you knavish Jew, you scurvy Israelite, you think you are worthy of honor."

Rashi raised his eyes to the duke's contemptuous features and shifted to the gaze of the bishop, a face worn with hard travelling.

"Bishop," the duke said, "even in your native Olmütz, I am

sure that you have never met a Jew who arrogated such honor to himself!"

Rashi looked at the bishop's face with misgiving. Could it be . . . ?

There were cries in the street. "The Jews! Burn their stores! Grab their goods!"

Duke Vratislav chuckled. "You see, rabbi, you are important after all. I merely have to arrest you, and my patriotic countrymen are inspired to avenge themselves on your race, cursed to suffer and wander the earth in punishment for their eternal villainy."

"Bishop," Rashi said. "Do you remember me?"

The bishop looked at him blankly.

"In the fabulous lands of the east? When you fell ill with an Eastern malady? And I nursed you . . . ?"

"Can it be?" The bishop gazed at Rashi in amazement. "Are you . . . ? Yes, it is . . . !

Rashi's eyes filled with tears.

The bishop fell upon Rashi's shoulders and wept. Stepping back and taking Rashi's hands in his, he looked down at Rashi's manacles.

He turned to the duke. "Remove these chains!"

"But—what is going on here?"

"When I was travelling throughout the Orient . . ." Briefly, the bishop told the duke how Rashi had, years earlier, saved his life.

"Oh, very well!" said the duke. "Oskar!"

A gendarme with a red cap bobbing over his left ear stepped forward smartly. "Yes, sir!"

"Undo the prisoner's chains."

"Yes, sir!"

The gendarme saluted smartly. In moments, he had the chains off Rashi's wrists.

"Thank you, Duke Vratislav," Rashi declared, rubbing his

chafed wrists. "But now there is not a moment to be lost. I can hear the shouts of the mob rising against the Jews. I beg of you, now that the bishop has told you how I, a humble Jew, saved his life, call off the rioters and forestall all bloodshed."

"Well, I don't know," said Duke Vratislav. "Since they have already begun . . ."

"It will be more than a riot if you do nothing, lord," Rashi said. "It will be a pogrom."

"A pogrom!" the duke sniffed. "Still, since the protest has already begun, perhaps the people should be allowed to vent their wrath."

The bishop turned to the duke with pleading eyes. "Such a policy is fit for uncivilized countries whose rulers are weak and subject to the will of their subjects. But surely, such indecision is beneath a man of your character."

"You're right," Duke Vratislav said. "Only a miserable coward would resort to such equivocation. Oskar!"

The gendarme stepped forward.

"Yes, sir!"

"Call out the regiment and have them quell the rioters. Arrest all disturbers of the peace and have them brought to the dungeon."

"Yes, sir!" He saluted smartly and, bringing his heels down, spun around and marched briskly from the room.

Rashi remained many days in Prague. The duke honored him, making him an advisor in his palace, and the duke became as well a fast friend of the Jews. (Maimon)

One day, Rashi knew that it was time to return home. He still had his commentary on *Nach* to finish, twenty-three *mesechtos* to work on and a handful of others that were still incomplete.

As he rode on a carriage from Prague, escorted by the Jews of Prague, Rashi reflected on his adventures. He had been a wandering beggar; accompanied by royalty; and he had gained the loyalty of the Jewish people. Always, however, he had remained the same Rashi.

On the carriage floor, grains of sand shook up and down like gold. Outside, the people began to sing farewell.

13

Halachic Decisions

RASHI WAS *ROSH YESHIVAH* OF TROYES. IN THESE YEARS—THE MID 1070s—Rashi's great teachers, Rabbi Yitzchak Halevi and Rabbi Yitzchak ben Yehudah, passed away. But they left behind them other great *talmidei chachamim*.

Troyes slowly became known as an outstanding center of Torah learning. Among the outstanding students that came to learn under Rashi were two of his sons-in-law: Rabbi Meir ben Shmuel (married to Yocheved) and Rabbi Yehudah ben Nassan (married to Miriam).

Rashi was a loving teacher. In his letters, he would often refer to his students as "my beloved," "my brother," "my friend."

Once, his students accidentally allowed something forbidden by *halachah*. Rashi corrected them gently: "I am certain that just as even a *tzaddik's* animal doesn't cause

121

damage, certainly *tzaddikim* themselves don't cause damage. But from now, do not act in this way. And may our Rock guide us in the path of truth and goodness." (*Teshuvos Chachmei Tzarfas Velothar* 15)

Rashi allowed his students to discuss issues with him freely. In their writings, they would note, "We offered this explanation to our rabbi"; or "and in this way did we argue before our rabbi."

Once, a student engaged in a lengthy argument with Rashi. Finally, the student proved his point by quoting from a *sefer*, and Rashi concurred. (*Teshuvos Chachmei Tzarfas Velothar* 82)

More letters came to Rashi, asking his view on *halachic* matters. Many of the letters dealt with questions on such topics as *kashrus*, holidays, blessings and marriage. His correspondents were usually great *talmidei chachamim* from France or Lorraine. They were at times past colleagues, his own teachers, and former students.

Sometimes, Rashi preferred not to give a *halachic* decision. Once, when his students asked him about a certain *halachah*, "he said nothing, neither allowing nor forbidding it." (*Haoraah* 2:36)

Rashi was kind both in the tenor of his decisions and in his dealing with others. Once, someone who had had a falling-out with Rashi needed to ask him a question. Fearing that Rashi was angry at him, he didn't put his name to the letter. Rashi wrote back, "I know who it is who has written to me with this question, for I recognize his handwriting. He is afraid to mention his name because he thinks I am his enemy. But this is not so. I do not withhold from him my blessing that goodness may come to him."

When Rashi had to correct someone, he did so kindly. "When you brought your proof . . . my beloved friend, you didn't think things out properly . . . I believe that you confused what you had learned." (*Teshuvos Chachmei Tzarfas Velothar* 41).

At times Rashi would change his mind about a decision he had made: "I used to allow this matter until now, but I was mistaken"; "at any rate, I was mistaken in that explanation." (*Pardes* 239)

To a student, he wrote, "I was already asked regarding that point for a few years, and I erred in my answer. But now thank you, my brother. May you increase in strength. I have learned from your argument; I agree with you, and I retract my original position." (*Melo Chafnaim* 36)

Of course, when Rashi accused himself of having made a mistake, he was judging himself by a vastly higher standard than we can imagine.

Once, Rashi expressed his modesty in an answer to Rabbi Yaakov Duravel, who had questioned him on a complex *halachic* matter. "I am the humblest of people and too low to place my head next to the high, tall mountain . . . How did it occur to the elder rabbi, the head of all the princes of Yaakov, Rabbi Duravel, to turn to such a young person [as I] to solve this problem? My heart tells me that the reason is that he likes me and so he treats me kindly. He has come to have pleasure with his small son and to test me, an empty vessel, and perhaps I shall gain wisdom."

Rashi's path was one of love. "The Jewish prophets were men of compassion. They would influence the idol worshippers to abandon their evil, for G-d stretches out His hand to both the evil and the righteous." (*Tehillim* 2:10)

Rashi's *halachic* stance was often lenient. There were those who said that if people have taken on the custom of prohibiting something to themselves that is in essence allowed, one cannot issue a decision allowing it. Rashi said to this, "Such a position of those who are strict . . . holds in the case of ignoramuses and gentiles. But when we are talking of learned Jews, one may issue a decision allowing them what is [basically] allowed." (*Teshuvos Chachmei Tzarfas* 11)

But Rashi was firm when the occasion merited it. At times, he would give a reply that differed from the standard approach, and he would append the words, "And this matter should not be publicized." (*Mordechai Bava Metziah, Shlach, Chulin* 12) Or: "Just as I was taught this privately, I have also taught it privately." (*Pardes* 240) Once, he explained himself: "When one grudgingly grants *halachic* permission, people tend to think that the matter is freely allowed, and they act even more leniently." (*Pardes* 241)

One day a woman came to Rashi with a question about *Taanis Esther.*

The exact details of the case are not known. The following is a creative rendering of the case.

"Oh, I just don't care!" Shoshana shelled a pod and angrily threw the peas into the large pot.

"Now you look here, Shoshana," the cook said, basting a turkey before the open oven door. "What Mistress Yehudis says, you've got to do!"

"Well, I don't care! She's no right to tell me to travel on a fast day."

Scant minutes ago, Yehudis had swept into the kitchen, her crinoline skirts rustling over the stone floor. "Shoshana," she had said, "I want you to get ready to go next morning with me to my brother-in-law in Sens, so we can get there in good time for *Purim.*"

"But Mistress Yehudis," Shoshana had protested, "you know that since *Purim* is on *Shabbos* this year, we'll have to fast on Thursday. And I can't spend a whole day riding on a fast. You know about my shortness of breath, Mistress Yehudis."

Yehudis had pursed her lips. "Now Shoshana," she said, "don't take liberties with me."

Now Shoshana shelled another pod angrily and threw the peas into the pot. "Take liberties with her! Didn't I used to dandle her on my knee when she was just a little girl? And now she goes through the house like she's some kind of princess. I do declare, if I have to go travelling all day long tomorrow with my shortness of breath, I'll eat and fast instead on Friday."

"You can't fast on Friday!" the cook said. "You know you're never allowed to fast on a Friday!"

"Well, I'll go speak to Rabbi Shlomo Yitzchaki about it," Shoshana declared. "I'll show that Mistress Yehudis that she can't twist me around her little finger!"

Rashi answered Shoshana's question as follows: "*Taanis Esther* is not a regular public fast either rabbinically or from the Torah. It is, rather, a custom that the Jewish nation has accepted upon itself. Nevertheless, no one has the right to act differently, thereby separating himself from the community." (*Machzor Vitry*)

As Shoshana walked home, she passed a couple of stooped men.

A minute later there was a knock at Rashi's door. "Come in!" he said.

The two men stepped inside. "Great Rashi, we have come to ask, if we are not taking up your valuable time . . ."

"What do you wish to know?" Rashi asked.

"This year, since *Taanis Esther* falls on a Thursday, we are not keeping the *mitzvah* of having the fast right before the holiday. So we thought that we will fast on Thursday so as not to act differently from everyone else, and then we will fast on Friday as well, to make the fast next to the holiday."

The other man asked Rashi, "Is this a praiseworthy practice?"

"No, it is not," said Rashi. "Acting in this manner is also considered separating yourself from the community. Shlomo

Hamelech has said of people who do such things, 'The fool walks in darkness.' (*Koheles* 2:14) This fast is no more than a custom carried out as a remembrance. Yet you wish to treat it as strictly as if it had been given in the Torah." (*Machzor Vitry*)

As a general rule, Rashi defended the strength of *minhag*, custom.

Regarding certain *minhagim*, he wrote, "'Hear, my son, the teaching of your father' . . . It is pleasing to act in this way, like the good custom . . . People have not carried out all these customs without reason. They saw that it is a good custom. And so 'do not turn aside from it, right or left.'" (*Pardes* 57)

"If the Jews in exile are not prophets, they are at least sons of prophets," Rashi wrote. "So one should not change a good and fitting custom." (*Pardes* 1)

"It has been said," he wrote elsewhere, "that if a *halachah* is weakly supported in the *Gemara*, and you don't know to what direction it tends, you should go see how the people are acting . . . This is our custom regarding rabbinic commandments that we are not sure about. We have learned that the custom of the previous generations is Torah. As the verse teaches, 'Do not reject the Torah of your mother.'" (*Pardes* 174)

He protested sharply against *talmidei chachamim* who ran roughshod over tradition. "There are people who add and detract from Jewish customs . . . things that they did not receive . . . They think that they have found a place where they can be innovative. But they have only found a place to boast. They make up their own custom. It doesn't occur to them that for the sake of avoiding controversy they should change their own ideas and walk on a straight path." (*Pardes* 175)

Rashi even favored custom over what seemed to him to be a grammatical error: the blessing recited in the *Shemoneh Esrei* between *Rosh Hashanah* and *Yom Kippur: Hamelech*

Hamishpat. It should have read, *Melech Hamishpat.* But it was preferable to keep the first reading, since it was customary. (*Pardes*)

However, if Rashi was sure that a particular custom was flawed, he would write, "There was a certain custom in this city, and it was abolished." (*Haoraah* 2:38); and "therefore, it is a *mitzvah* to forget that *minhag* and cast it down." (*Haoraah* 2:1)

There was another custom that Rashi disfavored, one that also had to do with *Purim.*

The story behind this *teshuvah* might have gone something like this:

The bell clamored insistently. Yehudis swept to the front door, smiling brilliantly, and flung it open.

"A happy *Purim!*" It was Yosef and Shaindel. Behind them, their magnificent carriage waited in the street, the gentile chauffeur sitting ramrod straight in a white and red uniform.

"Now, Ettie, give Yehudis your *mishloach manos!*" Shaindy pushed her five-year-old girl ahead of her. The girl handed the *mishloach manos* to Yehudis.

The platter was piled with food in a pyramid two feet high, featuring a representation in marzipan of Mordechai riding his horse.

"It's lovely!" Yehudis couldn't admire it enough. "And I have a *mishloach manos* for you! Oh, Marie! Would you bring that special *mishloach manos* we made for Yosef and Shaindel?" And in a fierce whisper: "Write their names on the card and stick it on the plate!"

She turned back to the couple with a bright smile. "Happy *Purim!*"

Marie stepped out, holding the platter, a massive column of fruits, pastries, wines and candies cunningly set onto a crafted basket of grape vines.

"Thank you so much," Shaindel said. "It's lovely."

"Yes, it is," Yosef added.

Shaindel's face brightened. "By the way, we haven't given any *matanos le'evyonim* yet. May I give a little present to your Marie?"

"Of course, Shaindy, that would be most gracious of you! I'll take it to her." She glanced inquisitively into Shaindel's purse.

Shaindel pulled out a sterling silver bracelet and matching earrings with onyx stones carved into stars of David. "It's just a little thing that I don't wear any more!"

"Why, that is so courteous of you! Happy holiday!" Yehudis shut the door.

Shaindel and Yosef walked back to the carriage, Yosef craning his neck around the side of the mammoth *mishloach manos*. As they stepped to the carriage, a Jewish pauper approached them, his thin arm stretched out. "*Matanos le'evyonim?*"

Shaindel looked at Yosef in exasperation. "Oh, give him something to make him happy," she said. "I already gave that expensive jewelry to Marie."

"Please take a fruit off the platter," Yosef said. Grabbing the fruit furtively, the poor Jew tucked it into his robe and hurried off.

When Rashi heard that Jews were giving *matanos le'evyonim* in this fashion, he responded with passion.

"Some people have the custom of giving gifts on *Purim* to servants and maidservants who board with their Jewish masters. Such a person is robbing from the Jewish poor. He thinks that he has fulfilled the commandment of giving 'presents to the poor.' But he hasn't, for this commandment refers to helping a poor Jew. Better than he is one who throws a rock into the sea." (*Hagahos Maimoniyos, Purim*)

Pesach came, and *Chol Hamoed*. Now Rashi expressed

his compassion in a *halachically* ambiguous situation.

Again, the details behind the *teshuvah* are unknown, but they might have been something like this:

Chiya sat at the table, drinking wine. It was dry, and he felt it flowing against his throat and through his chest and belly.

"Give me some more wine," he said.

Chiya's wife held the jug in her hand. "You've been drinking too much."

"I have not been drinking too much," said Chiya. "Listen, Leibl." He turned to his son, who was sitting at the table. Leibl was looking down and playing with his fork. "Tomorrow, we'll go fishing. Your mother will make us some pancakes. We'll get some grasshoppers in a jar for bait, and we'll catch some trout in the creek."

Leibl didn't say anything.

Chiya poured himself another glass of wine.

"You're drinking too much, Chiya."

"A man's got a right to do what he wants, doesn't he?"

Leah turned her back. "You remember when we were newlyweds?" she said. "You weren't like that then."

"No," said Chiya.

He had felt the pain since early morning. It had come and gone. Sometimes he felt it riding up his arm. Now it was sitting heavy on his chest.

Chiya took another drink. "Leah."

"What is it, Chiya?"

"Do you remember our *sheva brachos*?" The pain came back again. It was like an old friend or an old devil.

Leah turned around. "Yes," she said. "Yes."

Chiya made a face. "I don't feel good tonight."

"You drink too much, Chiya."

"It's all right," said Chiya. "Tomorrow, I'll take Leibl fly-casting. That will be all right." In the Lorraine, he had gone fly-casting. He remembered the feel of the cold water against his thighs, the heavy pull of the fish against the line.

Leibl had stopped playing with the fork. "I'm going to sleep, Tatta."

"You get a good night's sleep," said Chiya. "Tomorrow I will show you how to catch a trout."

The whole night, the wind blew, good and strong. Chiya listened to the crunch of footsteps on the street. The weight lay heavy on his chest now. He dreamt he was with his father in the cold, still water outside Troyes, casting for trout. This time he was grown up, and Leibl was there too. He squeezed a flow of cold, purple wine from the wineskin. It sprayed against his teeth and filled his mouth. The wine spread against his chest, cool and good, and then it turned into a heavy weight. Chiya struggled in his sleep. Then he no longer fought against the weight, and his entire body relaxed. When he relaxed, he looked much younger.

The next morning, Chiya lay still in bed.

"Chiya?" Leah walked over to him. He looked asleep. "Chiya!" She turned around and ran into the other room. "Leibl! Run and get the doctor!"

But it was too late for a doctor.

In the afternoon, a brisk wind was blowing in the cemetery. The gravestones were clean and white, and the long grass shook in the wind.

Leah held a handkerchief against her mouth. Beside her stood Leibl and next to them ten other mourners. One of the mourners present was Rashi. They looked into the brown, moist soil of the neat, rectangular pit.

Two men came out of the cabin at the cemetery entrance, holding a stretcher. The *tallis* covering Chiya's body fluttered in the wind and rubbed against the tall grass.

One of the mourners started reciting: "The Rock, perfect are His acts, for all His ways are just. He is a G-d of faith, without injustice. He is righteous and straight."

Another man interrupted him. "Stop it," he said. "It's *Chol Hamoed*. There's no public mourning."

Rashi stepped forward. "This is not correct. *Tzidduk Hadin* is not a sign of public mourning. It is an acceptance of G-d's judgment." He continued reciting: "The Rock, perfect in all His acts. Who shall say to Him, What are You doing? He rules in the depths and in the heights."

Leah took Leibl's hand. In the distance, she saw the glint of the river. She held on to the boy, and he didn't pull his hand away.

Later, in Chiya's house, Leah and Leibl sat on low benches in stocking feet. Chiya's brother sat on a bench next to the doorway.

Rashi came to the door. He was silent at first. It was not a time for public mourning. But Rashi could not stay quiet. What consolation do the mourners have in silence?

He began to speak to the mourners, consoling them. He eased their hearts.

One of the men leaned over and cried. He cried long and hard. Rashi did not stop him. It was a clean, healthy weeping. It would do the man good.

14

The Pope's Declaration

YEARS PASSED, GOOD, QUIET YEARS. RASHI'S LIFE CONTINUED WITH a regular tranquility: his work in the *yeshivah*, his income as manager of a vineyard.

Rashi's family was growing. Yocheved, married to Rabbi Meir ben Shmuel, gave birth to a son. His parents named him Shmuel.

One event marred Rashi's domestic peace. His third daughter, Rachel was divorced from her husband Eliezer. (*Sefer Hayashar Lerabbeinu Tam*)

Rashi had another sadness in his life. So busy had he been that since his last trip to Worms, he had never again had the opportunity to go there and meet with his teachers. For about twenty-five years, he wrote in one letter, he had had to deny himself the opportunity of visiting them.

Worms was only a few days' journey from Troyes. But

Rashi had been extraordinarily busy writing the huge mass of material that his commentaries comprise, running his *yeshivah*, acting as head of the community and answering questions from many other communities, as well as managing a vineyard.

One evening in April, 1095, tens of thousands of people across Europe watched an uncanny shower of meteorites. Peasant, nobleman, priest and artisan, Jew and Christian wondered what this almost supernatural sign meant.

Night after night, the silent shower of brilliant stars flaring from nothingness and blinking out into the dark sky continued.

What did G-d intend?

In the city of Lisieux, Normandy (in the northwest of France), Bishop Gislebert declared G-d's mind: He desired a Crusade, a holy odyssey, to the Christian holy sites in the East. Pilgrims had been returning from the Holy Land with news of shocking blasphemies, telling how the Muslim rulers had desecrated the holy sites of Christendom.

Seven months later, Pope Urban II convened the Council of Clermont, in Auvergne (150 miles northwest of Troyes).

On a cold afternoon, he stood on a platform before a sea of faithful Christians. Among them were more than two hundred high church officials, as well as princes and peasants, knights and barons. Cardinals stood near him in purple, bishops in gold, and monks in hooded cloaks. There were lords' ladies dressed in white kirtles with embroidered hoods, surrounded by their maidservants.

Across the broad field, tents and shelters had been erected, for the thousands of knights and common folk.

Above Pope Urban's head fluttered a cloth-of-gold canopy. At each end of the platform stood a figure in white, with white gloves, holding up a cross. Behind Pope Urban fluttered a gonfalon, a red, gold and white banner.

He was fifty-three years old, bald except for tufts of white hair above his ears, with a long beard and thick moustache. He was robust, with a stern, determined look. He wore a white robe, covered by a woollen vestment that lapped over his chest and back. This silver pallium was studded with tiny crosses.

The pope made a religious gesture, murmured a prayer, and began to speak. The crowd thrilled at his first words, for he spoke not Latin, the language of the Church, but their own French. He was the emblem of the Church, but he was also their man, a man of the people! His strong voice resounded throughout the vast field.

"Men of France!" his voice rang out. "You who are chosen and beloved by our god! You who have achieved so much! You who are outstanding in your faith and in the honor of our holy church!

"Men of France, today we call for a Truce of G-d! Across this land, Christian wages war against Christian, believer raises hand against believer. This land, favored by Heaven, has become an arena of skirmish, violence and enmity. We therefore declare, in the name of the faith and the Church: There shall be no fighting of any kind whatsoever from Sundays to Wednesdays. Nor shall there be fighting upon religious holidays. And there shall never be seen a raised hand among priests, monks, women, laborers and merchants."

Thousands of men listened silently. They knew from personal experience of the endless skirmishes and fights of the barons and knights, which had terrorized the countryside. Now the pope was at last addressing the problem.

"Men of France! There are princes in your favored country who raise sword against their neighbors; sack their towns, attack their goods and kill their people. Princes raise their hand against brothers; barons draw the sword against cousins. This behavior must stop! Knights of Europe: cease your bickering! Only the Church may declare war; only the Church has the power, in the name of our lord, to determine power.

"Men of France! Distressing news has reached our ears. Evil tidings have gone forth from Jerusalem and reached us from Constantinople. A horde has erupted from Persia, an accursed race, a people hated by G-d, a generation with a twisted heart and wayward spirit. These barbarous people, a multitude of Turks and Arabs, have invaded the lands of the Christians in the East and devastated them with sword, pillage and fire. They have advanced through the empire of Constantinople, reaching the Mediterranean Sea. Constantinople, which had been a Christian rampart, is now all but lost."

The crowd listened with dismay.

"Some Christians have been taken as captives to the cursed land of Persia. The Persians have laid hands on others and tortured them to death.

"There is no end to the vile torments that these infidels have devised. They have violated our churches and transformed them into mosques. Our altars have been defiled and smeared with human waste.

"Christians have been circumcised. Their blood has been smeared upon the altars and spilled into the baptismal fonts. Church naves serve as horse stables.

"These barbarous, sinful Persians have slit the bellies of Christians and drawn out the ends of their intestines, which they tied to a stake. They flogged the suffering Christian and forced him to circle the stake until his intestines were drawn out of his body and he fell dead to the ground. Other of our fellow believers were tormented in equally vile and evil ways: shot with arrows or their heads cut off with naked swords. And what shall I say of the abominations committed against our women? On this subject, it may be worse to speak than to remain silent."

A murmur arose amidst the thousands of listeners as the blood boiled within them.

"You know that the Muslim infidel has already extended his rule to the south of Spain. How long, men of France, before he marches through fair France, violating your wives and driving your children out as slaves?

"The Muslim heretics have tormented even the impoverished Christian pilgrim. They have humiliated him, taxed him cruelly, unfairly imprisoned and searched him, even cutting the calluses of his feet to see that he hid no treasure there. Pilgrims have been given bitter drink until they vomited or burst their bowels, to see if they had not swallowed coins. Men of France, I am speaking of your brothers, fellow-children of our church!

"Now listen to my message, you mighty race of men. You are the people that G-d has given might and glory in arms; you have been given courage and strength. Who else will take up the cause of vengeance, my brothers, if not you? Rise up, my brothers, and fling to the ground the long-haired heads of those who fight against you.

"Men of France, remember Charlemagne! Remember his valiant son Louis! Recall all the kings who destroyed the edifices of the pagans and in their lands established the holy church. The pagans hold our most holy sites and defile them with their unclean hands. Men of France, can you withhold yourselves from vengeance? Do not dishonor Charlemagne! Do not disgrace your heritage!"

Some men wept, others trembled, still others grasped their staves, ready to avenge themselves within the moment.

Pope Urban turned to look at the princes whom he had summoned, standing arrayed before him.

"Christian warriors, you are arrogant with pride! You turn upon your brothers, cutting each other down with the steel of the sword. Is this the service of our god? You are oppressors of children, despoilers of widows, wreakers of sacrilege, murderers awaiting the payment of blood. Like vultures that spot a corpse from afar, you rush to battle.

"Warriors, if you would save your souls, lay down the cudgel of such a knighthood.

"Come forward to the defense of our church. You who have engaged in feuds, battle the infidel. You who have been thieves, become soldiers. You who have served for a few coins, earn everlasting life.

"You shall triumph over your enemies, and the kingdoms of the East shall be your reward.

"Even if you will be conquered, you will have the glory of dying on the ground where our god died. He will never forget that you rose to him from the blessed battalions.

"Let no obstacle turn you aside. Arrange your affairs. In the winter prepare, and after the spring harvest, march on a holy pilgrimage to redeem the holy sites.

"The time has come, men of a mighty nation, to prove that you are moved by courage. The time has come to atone for the violence committed in a peaceful land. The time has come to make penance for victories won at the expense of justice and humanity.

"Hear me, loyal Christians!" Pope Urban raised his hands above his head. "If you must have blood, then bathe in the blood of the infidels!

"Soldiers of Hell, become true soldiers of G-d!"

The crowd was silent. Men strained to hear, their faces ablaze.

Pope Urban II put down his arms. "Let the old and infirm remain here on their soil. Let no woman set out on this holy crusade without a husband, brother or guardian, so that she does not become a hindrance. Let the rich who choose not to come aid the poor.

"But as for those of you who go: let nothing detain you: not

137

possessions nor your children nor your parents. Forsake your houses! Forsake your brothers and sisters! Forsake your fathers and mothers! Forsake your sons and daughters! March forward bravely, in the name of the Church! Thus shall you be gathered up into the everlasting reward of our savior!"

A man cried out: "*Dieu li volt! G*-d wills it!" Again he cried hoarsely, "G-d wills it!"

The crowd took up the chant, raising their hands, calling out in a roar. "G-d wills it! G-d wills it! G-d wills it! G-d wills it!" Their faces were red, their eyes blazing with fierce salvation. A transcendent exaltation swept through the field. It could be done. They would be the army of G-d to redeem the holy lands. More—to redeem the world. The men were burning with hope, with mission. A spark flashed in their hearts—and the first Crusade was born.

Pope Urban raised his hands. "Brothers! You would not speak these words had you not been inspired by Heaven. Yes! G-d wills it! These are the words of Heaven. G-d wills it! This shall be your war cry. G-d wills it! Proclaim these words wherever you go. Cast them into the face of the heathen foe."

Pope Urban raised up a small cloth crucifix.

"Brothers! Our god has come from his tomb to give you this cross. Wear it upon your shoulders and your helmets. It will give you the assurance of victory or the glory of martyrdom. It will be a reminder that our god died for you and that it is your duty to die for him!"

"G-d wills it! G-d wills it!" the crowd roared.

"Go! Do not fear! Your possessions will be safeguarded, and you will despoil the enemy of greater treasures.

"Do not fear death, for all who die on this holy crusade, whether or not in battle, shall have their sins forgiven.

"Do not fear torture, for in torture is the crown of martyrdom.

"Take up your sword and spear! Take up your halberd and

arrow! Take up your shield and helmet! Better to fall in battle than to watch the sorrow of your people. Better to die in blood than to see the desecration of your holy places.

"Go! Go in faith and confidence, for your army shall be led by no officer or prince but by our god himself!"

Pope Urban stepped back.

Cardinal Gregorio dei Guidone stepped forward, wearing a purple robe, and pronounced the general confession. The crowd fell upon their knees, beat their breasts and confessed their sins, and Pope Urban II made the sign of absolution above their heads.

A burly man came up to the podium: Adhémar of Monteil, bishop of Le Puy. Pope Urban bestowed upon him the leadership of the Crusading army, and gave him the cloth crucifix to affix to the right shoulder of his mantle.

This small cross and the slogan, "G-d wills it!" would become the electrifying symbols of the great Crusade.

Evening fell and the church bells rang, summoning the faithful to vespers. Men spoke among each other excitedly. Some told that they had seen in the eastern sky a vision of the city of Jerusalem.

Candlelight shone from the embrasures of the abbey room where Pope Urban stood in thought. Earlier in the year, the emperor of Byzantium, a city to the west of Turkey, had invited Pope Urban to send soldiers against the Muslim Turks. Now Pope Urban was providing that army. Byzantium had been drifting from the control of Rome, and now it would be brought in check. Thus, the Crusades would achieve two goals at one time.

In the hostels and tents, men and women excitedly sewed red crosses to their garments. Knights strapped on their swords. For the first time, pilgrims would be allowed—no, commanded!—to bear arms.

Pope Urban continued travelling across France. He held

conferences in Nimes in the south, and Tours and Rouen in the north, exhorting the people to leave behind family and home for the sake of holy battle, an army of peasants and princes under the command of Bishop Adhémar.

People gathered recruits for the coming battle of salvation, travelling throughout France and as far away as Scotland and Denmark.

Pope Urban II's call for a Crusade gave Christendom an aggressiveness that it had never had before. His call began two hundred years of bloodshed, murder and savage persecution of the Jews. The cyclone of violence that this Crusade unleashed would swirl through the centuries to our present age.

Pope Urban II had not called for such violence. He had told the people to set out on August 15 on a pilgrimage to the East, to battle against the infidel Muslims.

But the people could not restrain themselves. There were among them the credulous and the fanatic, thieves and vagabonds. Some went to fight for the love of their religion, others in order to escape the misery of their lives, and many for whom both goals were intertwined.

Under the guidance of other leaders of the first Crusade, these mobs were swept into a passion of violence and murder, particularly against the Jews.

Within a few months, they would massacre tens of thousands of Jews in the cities of the Lorraine: Mainz, Worms, Speyer and others. Many *talmidei chachamim* would be martyred. The *yeshivos* of Lorraine where Rashi had learned would be all but destroyed. Sometimes church officials aided the mobs and would betray the Jews; other times, Christians would defend the Jews and bring the murderers to justice.

The impassioned call of Pope Urban II for the liberation of the East would become the occasion of one of the greatest tragedies in the history of the Jews.

15

Rashi: Man of Halachah

THE NEWS OF THE CRUSADE SOON REACHED TROYES. ENTHUSIASTS rushed through the streets, red crucifixes affixed to their sleeves, and the church bells rang more vigorously and often than ever.

For the Jews, life continued as before. For some, that meant that their troubles continued. When that trouble could be *halachically* adjudicated, they would turn to Rashi.

Here is the creatively reconstructed background of a situation that was addressed by Rashi:

"Yedidiah!"

Downstairs, Yedidiah's older brothers, Yechezkel and Meir, were waiting. Yedidiah was thirteen years old; his brothers, twenty-three and twenty-five.

"Come on!"

"Where are we going?" he called down, leaping up from

bed and running to the window.

"You'll see!"

"I didn't *daven* yet."

"You can pray when you get there."

"Will there be a *minyan*?"

Yechezkel smirked. "You're a pious one, aren't you?"

They walked down the country lane for over an hour until they came to a hovel. A cur ran at them, waving its tail close to the ground and barking.

A man with white, disheveled hair limped out from the leaning door and squinted into the sun. "Who is it?" Only a few yellow teeth stood in his mouth.

"Yechezkel and Meir. We brought you the boy."

"What is this?" Yedidiah asked.

"You go with him." Yechezkel thumped him on the back. "You'll earn your keep here. We can't afford you in the city, doing nothing."

"Yechezkel! Meir!" Tears sprang into Yedidiah's eyes.

"Come here, boy!" the old man called.

"He's calling you. Go!"

"Come here, boy!"

Yechezkel and Meir walked back down the country road. Yedidiah looked after them. What should he do?

The dog yapped at his feet.

"I—I didn't *daven* yet."

"No time for that now, boy! You come here, or I'll show you what you get!" The old man lifted his hand as though to smack Yedidiah back-handedly. The muscles stood out on his neck, and his forearm looked thick and powerful.

"Yes, sir!" Yedidiah followed him to a barn behind the house, where a cow stood in its own filth, its ribs showing.

Yedidiah's parents had died within a month of each other. His father had been a merchant. His mother had been a small, pale woman who had loved Yedidiah and cried with him. But she never defended him against his father's blows.

The farmer pointed out a pitted wooden bucket. "Milk the cow and bring the bucket into the back of the house."

He turned about and stumped back to the house.

Yedidiah picked up the bucket and took a step to the cow.

A small, wooden stool stood next to the cow. Gingerly, Yedidiah sat on the stool and put the bucket below the cow's udder. He gave an experimental pull. Milk dribbled out. Good! He pulled more strongly. A stream of white splashed into the bucket. That wasn't hard! He pulled yet more confidently. There was a blur in the corner of his eye. Yedidiah leaped back and saw the cow's leg kick past where his chest had been a moment ago. The bucket fell over, and the milk dripped into the ground. Yedidiah looked down at his feet. His shoes and pants were smeared with filth.

From the house came the slam of the door, and the old man's voice. "You fool, what are you playing at?"

When Yedidiah's brothers had attended to the will, he hadn't been involved. They had said that they would take care of things for him. Soon they had said they could no longer allow him to learn—to sponge off them. He had seen how they filled their apartments with costly silver, how their wives wore jeweled barrettes, how their clothing turned from muslin to silk. He could no longer stay with them, for they could not afford him; he must earn his own keep; and so he had been given a shoddy room, a hovel; and now—

There was a smack against the back of his head; he stumbled into the filth. "You spilled the milk, you miserable boy! Now get back there with the bucket!"

Yedidiah managed to bring in half a bucket of milk. The little dog bit at his calves even as he carried the bucket in.

"Now this morning, you're going to weed the vegetable rows. I'll be out in the field plowing. You won't be out of my sight."

As Yedidiah crouched over the vegetables under the hot sun, he watched the farmer in the distance behind the cow, holding a wooden plow.

When the man disappeared behind a ridge, Yedidiah leaped up from the vegetable rows and ran to the house.

The dog ran out to Yedidiah, barking fiercely. Terrified, he picked up a stick. The dog lunged, and Yedidiah cracked the stick against the side of the dog's head. The dog yelped in mid-air, fell to the ground and backed away, whimpering.

"Hey, boy! Hey, boy!"

In the field, the farmer was running back to the house.

Yedidiah ran onto the road. He was thirsty, dizzy from the sun and already out of breath.

Desperately, he ran down the road, back to Troyes. Soon he was passing other farmers, Jews taking care of the vines.

The yellow fields and blue sky spun about Yedidiah dizzily, and a powerful hand grabbed him by the shoulder. So he had been caught! As he felt himself drift into insensibility, he heard a voice: "Boy, you're going to be sick." The next thing he knew, he was opening his eyes under the shadowy branches of an apple tree and a young, Jewish farmhand was pressing a wet towel across his forehead.

In the late afternoon, the farmhand, whose name was Jon, took Yedidiah back to Troyes with him. "You've got to see Rashi, the *rosh yeshivah*. What happened to you is outrageous. No one should take advantage of a child."

They went to the *beis midrash* and after *Maariv*, Jon accompanied Yedidiah to Rashi.

After Rashi heard the boy's story, he replied, "Usually, I reply to *talmidei chachamim* and do not get directly involved in disputes. But in this case, it is clear that you have been robbed by the other inheritors. It appears that your brothers have misused the *beis din* in order to take away that which Heaven gave to you. This is not even a legal question.

"Therefore, in this case I will advise you how to defend yourself. You will go back to the *beis din* and have them appoint a person to take care of you—"

"I'll do that," Jon broke in.

"Yes, take care of the boy," Rashi said. "But that isn't what I meant. The boy needs an *apitrofos*—a legal guardian who will be able to argue on his behalf."

"In the meantime, he can stay with me?"

"If he wishes to."

"Yes, I want to!" said Yedidiah. He looked back at Jon, this man who had shown him care. (*Teshuvos Chachmei Tzarfas* 28)

There was another case that Rashi got involved in, a case that had originally been under the adjudication of a former student of his.

This is the imagined background of that case:

It was a French village, with a handful of Jews. Avigdor was an intense adolescent with long, awkward arms and legs. It was his intention to learn in *yeshivah* for several years and then go into business as a merchant. He believed that one should learn Torah, that one should work for a living and raise good children. He believed that one must be ethical, righteous and practical.

Avigdor was engaged to Sarah Rivkah. He had agreed to the engagement because Sarah Rivkah's father was, like his own, a well-off merchant. He had talked little with her, but was confident that they would build a true Jewish home together.

His father had agreed to a dowry for the bride, and this had been placed in the hands of Shimshon, also a merchant.

One morning, Avigdor went to visit Sarah Rivkah's father, Reb Yudl, to discuss his support while he would be learning in *yeshivah*.

Avigdor passed a room where Sarah Rivkah sat at a table

writing, and knocked at Reb Yudl's door.

"Come in!"

Reb Yudl looked up from his ledger. He was a tall, portly man. His face broke into a smile. "Ah, my future son-in-law. What brings you to honor my presence today?"

Before Avigdor could reply, Sarah Rivkah stepped into the room. "Papa! I want to read you my latest"—she noticed Avigdor, and looked down. "Oh . . . ! I'll come back later."

"No, Sarah Rivkah, come in. I want Avigdor to hear. I'm proud of you." He looked at Avigdor proudly. "You didn't know that my daughter is a gifted poet!"

"Very well, Papa." Sarah Rivkah stepped forward and cleared her throat. "It's called, 'Dance Like Antelope.'

> Hashem, please help my feet
> Dance like antelope,
> Shimmer like a meadow,
> Climb like boulders strewn on mountains.
> Please help my fingers
> Gesture like smoke,
> Open like harvested fields,
> Endure like the hills,
> Flicker like the surf,
> Clap together like a flock of ravens.
> Please help my mouth
> Sing like forests,
> Roar like caves,
> Plead like stars,
> Burst like a field of poppies.
> Please help me be
> Strong as a crag which can endure all battering—
> To serve You, Hashem."

"That's lovely, Sarah Rivkah," her father said.

The girl beamed.

Avigdor frowned. "I'm sorry, but I'm confused. What is this poem about?"

Reb Yudl turned to his daughter. "Maybe you can explain it, Sarah Rivkah."

Sarah Rivkah gazed down at the floor. "It's about wanting to serve Hashem," she said. "It's about telling Him that I want to be close to Him in every way."

"I still don't understand," Avigdor replied. "If that's all that the poem is about, why don't you just say: 'I want to serve Hashem'?"

Sarah Rivkah wrinkled her brow. "Because that's not poetry. Poetry shows how I *feel*; it makes *you* feel how I feel."

"I'm sorry," Avigdor said. "I just feel confused!"

"Thank you, Sarah Rivkah," her father told her.

The girl left the room.

There was a long silence. Finally, Reb Yudl asked Avigdor, "*Nu?* What did you come to see me about?"

Avigdor stood a few moments, his fingers tapping the tabletop. Then he burst out, "I'm sorry—I can't marry your daughter."

"Can't marry my daughter?" Rabbi Yudl replied in astonishment.

"This poetry she's writing. It doesn't make any sense."

"Because she writes poetry you can't marry her?"

"I have to think practically," Avigdor replied. "Is it likely that a person who spends her time writing such—stuff—will be a responsible wife and mother? And even if she will be, can she really fit into a community?"

"Avigdor," Reb Yudl said, his face livid, "perhaps you are underestimating my daughter—and the community. Remember: you are engaged to marry Sarah Rivkah!"

"I know that," Avigdor replied stoutly. "But when I got engaged to her, I never could have expected this!"

Avigdor went directly from Reb Yudl's house to Rabbi

Mordechai in the *beis midrash*. Rabbi Mordechai had left the village ten years earlier to learn in Rashi's *yeshivah*. Now that he had come back, he was the rabbi of the community.

Rabbi Mordechai listened gravely to Avigdor's complaint. "I understand. You are a fine young man: serious, practical. You got engaged to a young woman whom you now see as flighty and over-imaginative. You can't relate to the things she talks about. I really don't see why you should be held to the initial agreement you made to marry her."

"And the dowry?"

"That should go back to your father."

"Thank you, rabbi," Avigdor said.

Rabbi Mordechai's decision caused an uproar in the community. Half the village supported Avigdor, and the other half said that he was shaming Sarah Rivkah.

Finally, a letter was sent to Rabbi Mordechai's teacher in Troyes, Rashi.

Rashi responded trenchantly:

"Regarding engagements, the earlier authorities have been accustomed not to shame a Jewish woman.

"Unless the groom agrees to take the woman as his wife, it will be lawful to punish him both financially and with lashes.

"As for my student who has supported the groom in his argument: you do not give honor to the Torah, for you are strengthening the hand of one who has done badly.

"From Heaven, your honor has been withheld. You have been withheld from understanding the obvious points of Torah. How much more will you not understand its depths.

"'To the rebukers will be sweetness, and upon them a blessing of goodness.' (*Mishlei* 24:25)" (*Teshuvos Chachmei Tzarfas* 27)

Another time, Rashi stepped in to put an end to a family feud.

Here is the imagined background to that case:

Yosef lived in an apartment sunk beneath the level of the street. From his window, he could see the footsteps of passers-by, carriage wheels and horses' legs.

Yosef had grown up a sullen, easily-hurt child. He imagined that every look given him was an insult, every comment a slur. It hurt him to have commerce with the Jews among whom he lived.

One summer, a new person moved into Cavaillon, a rotund man named Daniel, with white, curly hair and a clear gaze.

Daniel was a convivial man who soon became friends with many members of the community. And he also reached out to Yosef.

At first, Yosef would go to his house for a drink of schnapps. Then they began learning together.

Yosef visited Daniel a few times a week, and more and more he opened up his soul to him.

Daniel helped Yosef untangle his painful thoughts and emotions. Yosef no longer walked down the street expecting insults from everyone he passed. He engaged people in conversation at the market or on the street. Some didn't respond; but many others did. Yosef found that he was building a circle of acquaintances; even friends.

Yosef's parents had died some years ago. But he had some extended family. For years he had had little to do with them, but now their relationship began to bloom.

But the *gabbai* was not friendly. He never gave Yosef an *aliyah* to the Torah. On *Yom Kippur* and *Rosh Hashanah*, everyone had had a chance to draw aside the curtain of the *aron kodesh* at least two or three times before Yosef was called.

One *Shabbos* morning, Yosef walked up to the *gabbai* at the *bimah*. "I want to have an *aliyah* today."

The *gabbai* didn't look at him.

Yosef felt himself growing angry, and he raised his voice. "You never give me an *aliyah*. I want an *aliyah* today."

Without turning to look at him, the *gabbai* said, "You don't deserve it."

"I want an *aliyah*!"

It was turning into an argument. Other people became aware that something was going on.

The *gabbai* again said nothing.

"If you don't give me an *aliyah*, I want to know the reason why."

"I'll tell you why you don't get an *aliyah*!" The *gabbai* turned and faced Yosef, his face angry. His voice was raised. "I don't give you an *aliyah*, because you're a *sheigetz* and the son of a *sheigetz*!"

He turned back to the *bimah*, as though the matter was closed.

But there was an uproar from the shul.

"What's going on? Explain yourself!" a little man with a heavy voice shouted excitedly.

The *gabbai* turned back and pointed a trembling finger at Yosef. His face was crimson, and a vein on his temple pulsed.

"His great-grandparents were apostates!" He spit on the floor. "He's no more a Jew than the bishop. He doesn't belong in this *shul*."

The rabbi clapped his hand on the *bimah*. "G-d forbid that such a thing be said!"

Yosef looked at the rabbi. Thank goodness—someone was taking his part!

The rest of the *Shabbos* service went by quickly. The people were in an uproar.

By the end of *Shabbos*, everyone was talking about the controversy.

The *gabbai* no longer held back his bitter tongue. He

could at last expose the rancor that had eaten away at his heart. He went about telling everyone that Yosef was the grandson of apostates.

Someone recalled that there had been such a story, but they had done *teshuvah*, and become observant Jews again.

The *gabbai* continued spreading his accusation, and the argument broadened. The *gabbai's* family turned the matter into a family feud.

The rabbi held an emergency meeting. He declared that unless the *gabbai* and his family immediately desisted from their slander, they would be put into *cherem*—excommunication.

"I recall," said the rabbi, "that Rabbeinu Gershom himself decreed that no one may cast such insults against anyone else.

"Rabbeinu Gershom's own son was forcibly baptized. When the boy died, Rabbeinu Gershom mourned two weeks for him: one week for his body, and the other week for his soul."

The rabbi shook his head. "No one can say that he comes from such a good family that something like this cannot happen to him."

The *gabbai* had gathered his own meeting in his house. "They wish to make a *cherem* against us," the *gabbai* said. "So before they have a chance to do so, we will all take a vow that we refuse to accept any community decree."

He and his relatives found some statements in the *Gemara* that indicated that they could do this and outwit the *beis din*. Quickly, they vowed that they not be subject to any *cherem* pronounced against them.

The *gabbai* sent a learned note to the rabbi, telling him what he had done.

"This is an outrage!" the rabbi declared. He convened a *beis din* and put the *gabbai* and his family into *cherem*.

Other Jews in Cavaillon were confused by the *gabbai's*

references to the *Gemara* and the *Geonim*. Perhaps he had a point.

The rabbi decided to submit the controversy to Rashi, *rosh yeshivah* of Troyes.

In his answer, Rashi wrote:

"We have been warned from Sinai, 'No man may oppress his neighbor.' Our rabbis have said that this refers to oppressive and insulting words. If someone is a penitent, you may not tell him, 'Remember your former deeds.' If someone is a convert, you may not tell him, 'Remember the actions of your forefathers.' If the fathers sinned, the sons did not.

"The *gabbai* has no right to talk about the private lives of Yosef's grandparents. Repentance rises to the G-dly throne of glory. Our Sages tell us that even complete *tzaddikim* cannot stand where penitents stand. As the *pasuk* states, 'Peace, peace—both to the one who is distant and the one who is close.' (*Yeshayahu* 57:19)

"The vow that the *gabbai* and his family took is worthless. When they made the vow, they spoke a lie, for they vowed to transgress a *mitzvah* of heeding the voice of their community leader.

"The *gabbai* and his family deserve lashes for taking the vow. In addition, they are subject to the *cherem* that the community decreed against them." (*Teshuvos Chachmei Tzarfas* 21)

16

The Crusades Begin

POPE URBAN II'S MESSAGE OF REDEMPTION THROUGH HOLY BATTLE
raced through France. "Wait until summer, and then we shall
march in one organized movement."

But there were those who could not cool their burning
hearts. There were poor peasants, serfs who lived in constant
poverty who had no hope other than a brutish life, dying at the
age of thirty or forty, leaving behind squalling children who
too would be slaves to the lords.

There were bands of roaming beggars, tens of thousands
of men and women in despair—hungry, cold, sleeping in the
mud of a cold field or the corner of a reeking barn.

These men and women had lived in poverty, hopeless-
ness, pain. Now they could leave behind their wretched lives.
They could go on a march of glory that would be led by G-d
Himself. At the end of that march, they and their children after

them would live utterly transformed lives. Or, if they died, they would attain martyrdom and a death that assured them a place in Heaven.

Other preachers were spreading the message of the coming Crusade. But someone was needed to gather all these people, to ignite them and give them direction.

That man was Peter the Hermit.

It had already been some years since Peter had been marching through France and preaching about the need to free the Holy Sepulcher in Jerusalem from the Turks.

Peter believed with a burning faith in his mission. He had the power to sway crowds with his fiery rhetoric, and the confidence to lead them on a path that could be sustained by faith alone.

He was not a statesman or military man. He was a man of the people. When he spoke about the need to march eastward, it was not as Pope Urban to the princes and the burghers or even the peasants. He also spoke to the poor, the dispossessed, the thieves and vagabonds, the fallen men and women. He was in their eyes a saint, a mighty man of the spirit who recreated in himself the qualities of the Christian messiah.

He walked among the people barefoot, wearing a sleeveless cloak over a woolen, cowled smock, both reaching down to his bare feet. Words poured forth from his lips in a passionate, hypnotic torrent. They must go east to Jerusalem and redeem the Christian holy places. Everyone who went would be redeemed, his sins forgiven.

Peter was not a man of the flesh. Peasants were awed that he did not eat bread, subsisting on wine and fish. He was an extraordinary man, and peasants even plucked hairs from his mule as relics.

"Whatever he did or said, it seemed like something half divine," the monk-historian Guibert of Nogent, who knew

154

him personally, wrote of him.

He spoke spellbindingly about the vision he had had. He had seen the Nazarene himself in the Church of the Holy Sepulcher. The Nazarene had commanded him to gather the people and lead them against the infidel Turks. The Nazarene had promised that the gates of Paradise would open to all who took part in the holy crusade.

The people who listened to Peter the Hermit fell into convulsions of joy—weeping, dancing, raising their hands, crying out phrases of salvation.

Peter was not hampered by thoughts of strategy. He could not wait until the summer. Salvation awaited them now; the Nazarene wanted them in Jerusalem now; they must rely on their passion now.

Meanwhile, Pope Urban's planned Crusade was gathering so slowly that it would evidently not set out on time.

Indefatigably, Peter the Hermit preached his great vision and message. Apparently without consulting the Church, he announced that all those who wished to join the Crusade should meet in Cologne on Easter day, at the end of April.

Wherever he preached, men flung down their tools to follow him.

"Sell all you have if you must, gird your loins and join the Crusade of faith and salvation!"

The ardent peasants took Peter at his word.

Soon France was in economic turmoil. Everywhere, thousands of peasants were selling their most necessary possessions for pennies and paying inflated prices for provisions that they would need for the journey. These peasants, who had had the reputation of being the most stingy and miserly people in Europe, all but threw away their possessions to buy some fare for the road. They were on the trail of glory, and their end would be in glory.

"Each pilgrim was so bent on raising money, come what

may," Abbot Guibert of Nogent reported, "that he parted with his goods not at his own price but at the buyer's. So all men bought dear and sold cheap."

The peasants could not wait long. They had sold their farm implements, their artisan's tools. There was nothing more left for them here in France. They must travel soon, or else they would starve.

Peter the Hermit came from Amiens, a city one hundred miles northwest of Troyes. It was to Amiens that tens of thousands of beggars, peasants and vagabonds gathered to hear his electrifying messages.

Another message came forth from Amiens. This was an army of Christians setting out to battle the enemies of Christendom, the Muslims. But there were other infidels closer to home, who had murdered the Nazarene and, stiff-necked, turned their backs on eternal salvation, preferring instead their synagogues. The Crusaders were marching east-ward to overtake the enemy. But was it not ironic that here, living peaceably amongst them, the killers of the Nazarene were allowed to live serenely?

As this message was broadcast throughout France, the Jews were overcome by fear. No doubt Rashi in Troyes, a short distance from Amiens and along the general swathe that the Crusaders would go through on their way eastward, heard the bloodthirsty words being repeated among the fervent believers.

Many Jewish communities in France and Lorraine sent gifts to Peter the Hermit begging him to spare their commu-nities. Peter accepted these gifts.

The first attack on Jews took place in the city of Rouen, some fifty miles southwest of Peter's headquarters in Amiens.

The pious mob overran the Jewish quarter, seized the unarmed Jews and herded them down the narrow streets, pushing them into a church.

Other Jews were persuaded to enter the church by guile.

There, the leader of the pilgrims announced to the Jews: "Accursed Jews, killers of the Nazarene! You have the choice of dying like unsaved dogs or of accepting the faith of love and salvation.

"Come! Who will be the first to bend his head before the cross upon which the beloved redeemer died?"

No one moved.

"Stubborn Jews! Who will step up and bend the knee before the meek lamb of G-d, lest he turn into a wrathful deity?"

Among the Jews, silence. Murmurs, weeping, prayer.

A few Jews, their heads hung down, stepped up to the priest.

"Kneel and accept the Nazarene!"

They slowly knelt before the cross.

"Get them out of here!"

Two peasants armed with clubs hustled them out of the church.

"Who else shall stand up to accept our savior?"

There was silence.

"Who else?" the priest roared.

"*Shema Yisrael!*" a voice cried out.

Dozens of other voices, men, women, children, cried out piteously, "*Shema Yisrael!*"

The leader of the Christian faith signalled to his followers.

With a roar, taking knives, clubs and swords in their hands, they leaped upon the quivering Jews. There were cries, screams. Some Jews prayed. Others fought back with bare hands. Mothers bent over their children, fathers stood before their sons and daughters.

The carnage went on and on.

Then there was silence—just the joyous whoops of the pilgrims, ripping booty off the bodies. The Jews had been slaughtered—every one of them.

The march to the east, the sacred Crusade, had begun.

News of the massacre spread to the Jewish communities. A day of mourning and fasting was declared, and a warning letter was dispatched to the Jews of Speyer, Worms and Mainz. "Fast and seek mercy from G-d Who dwells on high so that you might be spared!"

But the Jews of Lorraine felt secure. Troubles and massacres might happen elsewhere—but surely not here in Germany.

The Jews of Lorraine sent a letter back to France:

"All the communities have decreed a fast day. And with this, we have done our duty. May the Omnipresent One save us and you from all trouble and affliction. We are greatly concerned about your well-being. As for ourselves, there is no great cause for fear. We have not heard a word about such matters, nor has it been hinted that our lives are threatened by the sword."

How these words have echoed throughout history! The Jews of Spain knew that trouble could strike in other countries, but as for themselves, there was no cause for fear—until 1391. The Jews of Poland were secure, in the highest echelons of society—until 1648. The Jews of Germany lived in the most civilized nation in the world—until 1939.

What an ironic, savage ring these words have, echoing through every country that Jews have lived in, through every century of the *galus*!

By March of 1096, ten thousand pilgrims from all the provinces of France had gathered in Amiens to follow the inspired hermit eastward. There were even Scotsmen, in short, fur tunics that left their knees bare, their baggage slung over their shoulders. The pilgrims who did not speak French showed that they too meant to join the Crusades by placing one index finger over the other in the shape of a cross. Men

and women, young and old. They had sold all their possessions for carts, horses, bedding and food.

Peter the Hermit circulated among them indefatigably, a
saint, a holy man.

Knights and burghers came before him, bearing gifts of
gold, horses and carriages. He accepted these graciously, as
an emperor. The same day, he would distribute the wealth to
the grateful poor.

Women of loose morals were among those who had
joined the throng. He redeemed them. Providing them with
dowries, he found them husbands and conducted marriages.

Where there was strife, he brought peace. Where there
was division, he brought about brotherhood.

All through the day, people sang hymns and played music,
as they would continue to do during the march. At night, they
slept beneath cloth roofs held up by posts.

In addition to the pilgrims, there had also gathered ten
thousand foot soldiers and a handful of men on horseback.

Peter had appointed five knights, all of the same family, to
act as military leaders: Walter de Poissy, a nobleman, and his
four nephews, Walter, William, Matthew and Simon.

In March, 1096, the throng began its epic voyage to
salvation.

The Jews of Lorraine had responded with self-assurance to
the warnings of the Jews of France. They were about to face
mass murder.

17

Holocaust

THE GREAT MASS OF THE PEOPLE'S CRUSADE MARCHED EASTWARD through France.

It is possible that some of these Crusaders marched through Troyes, where Rashi would have seen them.

A horseman pulled up before the throng and demanded to see Peter the Hermit. The crowd pointed him out. The horseman flung himself off his horse, approached the holy man deferentially, and handed him a missive from the Jews.

"This is a public letter from the Jews of France, my lord, to the Jews of all the communities that you shall pass through on your way to the Holy Land.

"The letter bids that they provide you with all the provisions you require, in consequence of which you shall not molest those communities and shall speak favorably on their behalf to all who might think to trouble them."

Peter the Hermit took the letter. "I shall abide by the provisions of this letter, if the Jews abide by the request of their compatriots."

Possibly, Peter the Hermit did restrain those people directly under him from attacking the Jews in return for provisions. But there were other companies of Crusaders led by bloody-minded commanders.

Now began a three months' reign of terror.

It was *Shabbos*—the eighth day of *Iyar*.

Mobs under the command of a man named Count Emich of Leiningen, burst into Speyer, city of *talmidei chachamim* and *yeshivos*. Joined by local Christians, the Crusaders fell upon the Jews.

Most of the Jews escaped, taking refuge in the palace of Bishop Johann. Whether out of altruism or because he had been bribed, Bishop Johann was a hero to the Jews.

The Crusaders captured twelve Jews—eleven men and a woman. "Accept the cross or die!"

The woman was the first to sanctify the Name of G-d, taking her life with her own hand.

The eleven other Jews refused the cross, and the Crusaders murdered them.

The mob stormed the Jews in the palace, but the bishop sent out armed men to protect them. Finally, capturing some of the Crusaders responsible for the murders, he had their hands cut off.

The Jews of Germany turned to G-d, "resorting to the custom of our ancestors: repentance, prayer and charity." (The Chronicle of Shlomo bar Shimshon, *The Jews and the Crusaders*) They fasted for three days and nights in a row and then fasted many consecutive days.

"But their Father did not answer them; He obstructed their prayers, concealing Himself in a cloud through which their prayers could not pass. He abhorred their tent and removed them from His sight." (*ibid.*)

Pope Urban II had preached a Crusade in which princes would channel their violent energies into consolidating the church's power and overcoming the Muslim hold on the Holy Places, thus ushering in the age of redemption.

Peter the Hermit had stressed a populist Crusade that would be fulfilled by the most despised and hopeless classes.

In Germany, the ideology of the Crusades took on a cruel, insane cast under the leadership of the ruthless Count Emich.

"There will be one Last Emperor who will fight the enemy of the Nazarene in Jerusalem. I am that Last Emperor. I will triumph, and my reign will last for a thousand years."

The thousand year empire! Were these not the words that Hitler, may his name be blotted out, used to describe his Third Reich?

"Before the Nazarene returns to earth, all the Jews shall be converted to Christianity. And so as I march East to bring about the Last Days, I shall offer the Jews the cross or the sword.

"Heaven has sent a wondrous sign confirming me, for upon the hair on my chest, a red cross has taken shape."

Soldiers and peasants from Flanders and far-away England flocked to gather behind this madman.

Emich was not interested in heading directly for the East. First, he must attend to the Jews.

He turned north, to the city of Worms.

Emich camped before the city and accepted the bribe that the Jews offered him. Then, on the twenty-third of *Iyar*, a rumor was spread that the Jews had killed a Christian, and Emich savagely attacked the city.

The Jews broke into two camps. One remained in their homes. The other ran to Bishop Adalbert's palace, seeking refuge.

"Those Jews who remained at home were set upon by the

steppe-wolves who pillaged men, women and infants, children and old people. They pulled down stairways and destroyed houses, looting and plundering. They took the Torah scroll, trampled it in the mud, and tore and burned it." (*ibid.*)

Seven days of terror for the surviving Jews in the bishop's palace passed. The new moon of *Sivan* arrived—the day upon which the Jews had arrived at Har Sinai to receive the Torah.

Emich's troops burst into the bishop's court. First, he demanded that the Jews convert, but they refused, and some Jews took their own lives.

Fathers slaughtered their children. Grooms slew their brides. Mothers killed their babies. The cries of "*Shema Yisrael*" rose to the Heavens.

Emich and his troops waded into the bloody scene and murdered the remaining Jews.

Then these brave and hardy soldiers, pious soldiers of G-d, stripped the bodies naked, still warm with their own blood, and threw them into the street.

A very small number chose to escape the carnage by accepting forced baptism.

About eight hundred Jews were murdered.

Among them was Rabbi Sasson, Worms' leading *talmid chacham* and *askan*, whom Emperor Henry IV had referred to as "Salmann, bishop of the Jews."

Rabbi Kalonymus ben Shabsai had come some thirty years earlier from Rome (a few years after the passing away of Rabbi Yaakov ben Yakar). He had been known as an extraordinary *talmid chacham* and writer of *piyutim*. He was also murdered.

The three sons of Rabbi Yitzchak Halevi, Rashi's teacher, had lived and taught in Worms. One of these sons was Rabbi Yaakov Halevi, also known as Rabbi Yaavetz, one of the greatest *talmidei chachamim* of the generation. They also died on this day.

His brother Rabbi Shmuel had been a leading *talmid chacham*. He too was no longer alive.

(The third son was Rabbi Eliezer.)

Following this glorious victory, Emich's troops marched northward to continue winning souls.

News of their exploits in Speyer swiftly reached the Jewish community of Mainz.

The rabble of Mainz, joined by some Crusaders, went to attack the Jews.

But other Christians defended the Jews. Soon, a pitched battle was going on between these two groups of Christians.

When a Crusader was slain, his allies started yelling that it was the Jews' fault and regrouped their forces.

The Crusaders were filled with righteous wrath. The Jews had dared to kill a Crusader!

The Jews abandoned their homes and took refuge in the court of the count and the bishop's chambers, going to synagogue only on the *Shabbos* before *Sivan*.

Two Jews reported that during the night, they had heard the wailing of souls in the synagogue. Hearing this, the Jews cried out to G-d, feeling that the decree had been sealed against them.

The Jews were on good terms with Archbishop Ruthard, and they bribed him and his officers with three hundred silver coins. Ruthard told the Jews to go into his palace courtyard, where he and his men would protect them.

"We shall die with you or remain alive with you!"

The Jews entered the bishop's courtyard, the men carrying armor and swords.

Rabbi Kalonymus, Parnas of Mainz, sent an urgent letter to King Henry, asking for protection.

King Henry immediately sent letters to his ministers commanding them not to harm the Jews and to provide them with help and refuge.

One of these men was Godfrey of Bouillon, duke of the lower Lorraine, who also was leading a division of Crusaders. He declared that he would not harm the Jews.

Count Emich arrived at Mainz on *Rosh Chodesh Sivan*, camping outside the city, where he remained for two days.

A messenger rode out to him, bearing a bribe from the Jews of seven pounds of gold.

The third day of *Sivan* came. At noon, Count Emich's troops marched to the town walls. Jew-haters defied Archbishop Ruthard and opened the gates, and Emich's troops poured in.

The Jews put on their armor and took their weapons in their hands. But their many days of suffering and their many fasts had weakened them.

Emich's troops overran Mainz and lay siege to the Jews in the bishop's quarter. They cried out for the blood of the bishop, who had protected the Jews.

The bishop, in fear for his life, disappeared. The troops that he had promised would protect the Jews withdrew.

The Jews were left alone.

The armed Jews rushed to the gate to defend themselves against the hordes of Crusaders.

But they were fearfully outnumbered. The enemy pushed at the gate and would soon be breaking through.

The Jews fell back. Together, they declared that before allowing the hands of the Crusaders to touch them, they would utter the blessing on sanctifying G-d's Name and sacrifice their lives.

Rabbi Menachem ben Yehudah spoke to the Jews passionately. "Be whole in your dedication to G-d. When Yaakov thought that his children might have a defect, they cried, '*Shema Yisrael!*' When the Jews received the Torah, they cried, 'We shall do and obey!' and '*Shema Yisrael!*' We are their children and what shall we say?"

The people cried out in a heartrending voice, "*Shema Yisrael!*"

"Anyone possessing a knife should examine it to see that it is not defective, and then let him slaughter us!"

The marauding Crusaders burst into the courtyard at last. There they found the *rosh yeshivah* of Mainz, Rabbi Yitzchak ben Rabbi Moshe, together with other *talmidei chachamim*, wrapped in their *talleisim*. The Crusaders grabbed Rabbi Yitzchak and decapitated him. His blood gushed onto the ground and his head, his lips which had spoken words of Torah, rolled in the dust.

The Crusaders hurled stones and shot arrows at the other men in the courtyard, who remained in their places. The emboldened Crusaders ran upon them with their swords and pierced them all.

Most of the Jews were hiding inside the palace chambers.

When they saw that the Crusaders had burst through the courtyard, they took knives in their hands to kill themselves.

Women killed their sons and daughters, and then turned the knives on themselves. Men killed their wives and children.

The streams of blood of man and wife, bridegroom and bride, student and teacher, mingled and flowed in the hellish scene of slaughter.

As the marauders rushed through the courtyard, women went to the windows and cast out silver and coins so as to keep the Crusaders preoccupied with gathering the money.

When the Crusaders finally burst into the chambers, they found the floors covered in blood, and the bodies of pure men, women and infants writhing in agony.

The heartless Crusaders stripped them of their clothes and money, and slaughtered whomever they found still alive.

One room, however, was well-barred, and the Crusaders could not break into it. But toward nightfall it became clear that the Crusaders would soon burst in.

Rather than allowing their children to fall into the hands of the Crusaders, the Jews took them and slaughtered them.

The women hurled stones onto the heads of the Crusaders from the window. The Crusaders threw stones back, grievously injuring the women.

But the women continued to stand at the windows, taunting the bloodthirsty Crusaders: "In whom do you place your trust? In a putrid corpse!"

When the Crusaders at last burst into the chamber, there was not one survivor.

They raised their pennants and rushed to another refuge of the Jews in the count's courtyard, and there they slaughtered as many Jews as they could.

The Jews retreated into the rooms, and the conquering Crusaders followed. Finding a Torah scroll, the Crusaders tore it apart.

When the Jewish women saw this, they called to their husbands, "Look, the enemy is tearing apart our Torah!"

The men rent their garments and then, accompanied by the women, stoned one of the Crusaders to death.

When the Crusaders and the local gentiles who were helping them saw that the Jews were fighting back, they broke into the room through the roof and threw stones and shot arrows at them.

There was a man there named Yaakov ben Sullam. The Jews had always treated him disrespectfully because his father was not of a distinguished family, and his mother was a convert. He cried out to the Jews, "You have always scorned me. But now look what I do!" He took a knife and drove it into his neck.

It was a bitter *galus* when Jews disrespected those whom they should most love.

The Crusaders, together with their local allies, went to seek new victories.

167

A priest was sheltering a family in his courtyard.

The mob surrounded the yard and yelled for the Jews to be baptized or murdered.

The priest went to David, the head of the household. "Listen. The mob has killed all the Jews in the bishop's and count's courtyards, except for a few who have consented to be baptized. I cannot hold these men back. Agree to baptism, and you will save your life, and the lives of your wife and children."

David replied, "Tell them to come here."

The priest ran out to the mob. "The Jew agrees to be baptized!"

Yelling in joy, the mob surrounded the room where David and his family had taken refuge. David stepped forward and spoke the words that he knew would be the last that he would speak on this earth. "You are the children of sin, for you believe in a god who was a *mamzer* and who was killed. But I believe in the everlasting G-d Who dwells in Heaven. If you kill me, my soul shall reside in Heaven. But you shall descend to the deep pit of hell, together with your god, and you shall suffer in boiling excrement forever!"

The frenzied mob charged into the house, murdered David and his family and threw their corpses from the windows.

There were other tales: people who had been forced into baptism who then gave up their lives to fire; women who sanctified G-d's Name with their lives.

There were also tales of resistance: of Rabbi Kalonymus, the outstanding *talmid chacham* who, after the bishop reneged on his promise to protect the Jews, tried to assassinate him with a knife, but was clubbed to death. There was a man named Shneur, who slew a gentile.

Over eleven hundred Jews died in the terrible slaughter. Among them died some of the world's leading Torah sages. With their death was destroyed one of the world's greatest centers of Torah learning.

Rabbi Shmuel Hakohen, prominent *talmid chacham*; Rabbi Yitzchak ben Moshe, *rosh yeshivah* in Mainz (mentioned earlier); Rabbi Menachem ben Rabbana David Halevi, community leader, famous as "one of the greatest men of the generation"—all murdered.

Afterwards, the townspeople who were relatively sympathetic to the Jews used the money that the Jews had entrusted with them to bury their corpses in a mass grave.

Bands of Crusaders roamed through Lorraine. Some peasants followed a goose, believing that it was divinely inspired. Others followed a black she-goat.

These were creatures sacred to the pagan tradition of Germany. As the peasants straggled behind, they sang old pagan songs.

A thousand years later, the Nazis would again enrapture their nation with the stirring myths of the pagan German spirit before it had become corrupted by Judaism.

The Crusaders continued northward, to Cologne.

They broke into the city on *Shavuos*. Finding the homes of the Jews deserted, they destroyed the synagogue and dragged its Torah scrolls into the street, where they unrolled them, threw them into the mud and rode over them.

A thousand years later, the Nazis would be making shoes of Torah scrolls.

The Jews hid in the homes of friendly Christian neighbors. Bishop Hermann III had groups of Jews taken out and hidden in surrounding villages and manors that belonged to him.

But immediately following the holiday, the butchery began, lasting until the eighth of *Tammuz*.

The Crusaders searched throughout Cologne and the surrounding villages. Wherever they found the Jews, they killed them. In Neuss, Welfinghausen, Xanten, Maerz, Geldern and Altenahr, Jews were slaughtered or took their own lives. Some Jews threw themselves on swords. Others drowned themselves. The rivers were reddened with their blood, the ground soaked with their blood.

Count Emich now turned east to Jerusalem, but his followers spread throughout the Moselle Valley, hunting down Jews.

In Eller, a young woman was placed by her father-in-law in the arms of her dead bridegroom, where he slaughtered her in the name of the Holy Blessed One.

In Xanten, the hordes fell upon the Jews on Friday night, as soon as the *Shabbos* meal had begun.

"Let us now recite the *Birkas Hamazon*. Afterwards, we shall slaughter ourselves, before the enemy can reach us," Rabbi Moshe, the head of the table, said. "Then we shall enter the eternal *Shabbos*. Each one of us will dine in the company of the *tzaddikim* with diadems of gold set with precious stones and pearls upon our heads."

The people answered, "*Amein*, so may it be His Will."

Rabbi Moshe began the *Birkas Hamazon*: "Let us all bless G-d of Whose bounty we have partaken."

"Blessed be our G-d of Whose bounty we have partaken . . ." the company responded.

Rabbi Moshe replied, "May the Merciful One avenge Your servants' blood . . . ; may He save us from wicked men, from forced conversion and from idolatry . . ." and he added many other benedictions.

Then, having finished the *Shabbos* meal, the people prepared to die.

A proselyte asked Rabbi Moshe, "If I slaughter myself for the sake of G-d, what shall become of me?"

Rabbi Moshe replied, "You will abide with us in our company and dwell with our father Avraham, who was the first proselyte."

When the proselyte heard this, he took the knife and killed himself.

When the Crusaders invaded the town, they found everyone dead. In their terror they fled, and the gentile towns-people came and buried the martyrs.

In Mehr, the mayor had promised to protect the Jews. But when the Crusaders swarmed over the city, he told the Jews, "I can no longer protect you. If you do not surrender to baptism, the enemy will attack and destroy the entire city. I would rather hand you over and save the rest."

But the Jews refused.

The mayor led them out to gaze upon the multitude of the Crusaders, camped at the wall of the town.

But the Jews would not be baptized.

In order to prevent the Jews from slaughtering each other, they were imprisoned separately. The next day, they were delivered into the hands of the Crusaders. The Crusaders killed some of the Jews and forcibly converted others.

A man named Shemariah escaped with his family, but the bishop's bursar, who had taken a large sum of silver to save him, delivered him into the hands of the villagers of Tremonia.

Shemariah pleaded that he and his family be allowed to spend one more night as Jews before converting.

That night, he killed his wife and three sons and then turned the knife upon himself, but fainted before he could die.

The next day, Shemariah refused baptism. The villagers forced him to enter a pit with his three dead sons on his left and his wife on the right, and they buried him alive.

A thousand years later, the Nazis too would bury Jews alive in mass graves.

For twenty-four hours, Shemariah shrieked and wept.

The next day, the Christians pulled him out and insisted that he convert. Again, he refused, and he was again buried alive until, mercifully, he died.

In Trier, the Jews gave all they had to the bishop to guard their lives.

The bishop gave a sermon speaking in the Jews' favor, and the Crusaders decided to murder him. He fled into the church and hid for a week.

He then went to the Jews and told them, "I can no longer help you."

"Did you not promise to protect us until the king returned [from Italy]?"

"Know that even the king himself could not deliver you from the hands of these Crusaders. Therefore, convert or you shall die."

The Jews asked that the bishop give them four days' reprieve until *Shavuos* passed.

The bishop did so. He intended to kill two or three Jews to weaken the hearts of the others and cause them to accept conversion. In this manner, he hoped to save his own life from the Crusaders.

The Jews were surrounded and kept from killing themselves. Some were murdered, and the rest forcibly converted.

In Metz, twenty-two people were slaughtered, and the others forcibly converted.

In Regensberg, the entire community was brought to the river and forcibly baptized.

In Sla, the Jews were saved. They had requested three days' grace before either baptizing or dying. In the meantime, the duke sent a thousand swordsmen to protect them. Also, among the Jews themselves were five hundred young men who bore arms. In the ensuing battle, only six Jews were killed, and many Crusaders and townspeople who fought with the Crusaders lost their lives.

Another branch of the Crusaders, led by a German named Gottschalk, also killed Jews. And a German named Volkmar led his Crusaders eastward into Hungary where, in Prague, the Jews were either forcibly converted or murdered.

Almost none of these ragtag Crusaders who had massacred the Jews reached the Holy Land. As they marched eastward, they attacked the cities of Hungary and were in turn set upon and massacred.

So vile had their excesses against the Jews been that in retrospect, even Christian historians attributed their failure to reach the Holy Land to the punishment of G-d. "After the atrocities they had committed," wrote the Christian historian Albert of Aachen, ". . . this whole intolerable company of men and women, laden with Jewish booty, continued their journey to Jerusalem and marched toward Hungary," where they were wiped out. "All this was surely G-d's Hand against the pilgrims who had sinned before His face with lechery and shamelessness, and who had slaughtered the homeless Jews, enemies of the Nazarene though they are, more out of greed than fear of G-d."

The reign of terror had begun in May and ended at last in July. Twelve thousand Jews had died.

It was more than a slaughter of individuals or even of communities.

It was the destruction of many of the greatest *talmidei chachamim* and the greatest *yeshivos*, of a tradition that could not be reconstructed.

There had been nothing comparable since the destruction of the *Beis Hamikdash*.

"That day the diadem of Israel fell, the students of the Torah fell and the outstanding scholars passed away . . . Gone were the sin-fearers, gone were the men of virtuous deed; ended were the radiance of wisdom and purity and abstinence . . . Gone was truth; gone were the explicators of the Word and the Law; fallen were the people of eminence and the sage . . . Since the day on which the Second *Beis*

Hamikdash was destroyed, their like had not arisen, nor shall there be their like again." (*ibid.*)

There was another facet to this tragedy: it was the first step in a new level of Christian violence against Jews. The church itself would gradually come to acquiesce in such murders. The persecutions would continue and become part of the doctrine taught by such Christian leaders as Martin Luther. At last, this hatred would blossom into the holocaust.

18

Mourning and Rebirth

REMOVE YOUR WRATH, QUIET AND SOOTHE YOUR ANGER.
No one can stand; the tragedy has grown.
Yaakov, small and humble, cannot come before you in
    judgment.
He seeks Your favor, charitable G-d, in his poverty.

The hewn stone fell, bricks and mortar that we had joined
    together,
The cedars were cut down; the sycamores we had put up
    were exchanged.
We are a generation that lacks someone to pray for us; we
    turned aside, we were blown away,
We were pursued, sins hung about our necks . . .

We have trusted in You, in Your salvation; G-d, raise us,

RASHI

Be merciful, remove Your anger, return to us,
We have hoped to take refuge in Your shadow;
Bring us close, for we have hoped for You; in You our heart
   rejoices.

In his *selichos*, Rashi poured out his grief at the tragedy
that had overtaken the Jewish people.

He mourned for the death of over ten thousand Jews.

He mourned for the death of the communities where he
had been a student.

He mourned for the destruction of the great institutions of
Torah that had been destroyed.

Seven of Rashi's *selichos* still exist. One of them, *Hashem
Elokei Hatzivakos*, is recited on the eve of *Rosh Hashanah*.
Another, *Az Terem Nimtachu*, is said on *Tzom Gedaliah*.

In one of his *selichos*, he addressed the Torah scrolls that
had been desecrated and torn apart by the mobs.

Perfect Torah,
Preceding the world by a thousand years,
Plead before G-d
On behalf of the blameless dove.

Stand in prayer
Before G-d in Heaven
That He have mercy on those who learn you
At every moment and season . . .

Is there no Yeshurun
To sing your song?
You have been silenced
From every mouth and throat.

Who will nurse from your breasts,

Who will rejoice in your pleasures,
If the throats of those who learned you
Have been silenced and strangled?

Approach with pleading
The face of the Eternal Helper.
Wrap yourself in black
Like a woman in mourning.

Seek out the insult of your pious ones
And the spilled blood of those who learned you.
From the hands of the low-born
Who murdered your students,

Who tore your parchment
And trampled your letters,
Who in blazing fury
Destroyed your synagogues.

Ask of the Awesome One
That He heal and redeem us,
That from among those who anger Him
He gathers His dispersed people.

In commemoration of the awful massacres, the Jews of
France ordered fasting and public mourning, at which time
these *selichos* were publicly recited.

The massacres of the Crusades also made their mark in
Rashi's *teshuvos*. In one *teshuvah*, he refers to a woman
whose husband "was killed on the day of the great bloodshed." (*Elfenbein*)

Some of his comments on *Nach* also seem colored with
the experiences of the destruction. Yeshiyahu (53:9) proph-
esied, "His grave was placed among the evil, and with the

wealthy his tomb. Although he had committed no violence, and had spoken no deceit."

Rashi commented, "He gave himself over to be buried in any way that the wicked idolaters would command, who inflicted upon them death and 'a donkey's burial in a dog's belly.'

"He agreed to [such] a burial rather than deny the living G-d. In keeping with the decision of the ruling authority, he gave himself over to all sorts of death decreed against him because he didn't want to do evil and violence, as was done by the idol worshippers in whose midst he lived."

After the massacres, the *yeshivos* of the Lorraine were reconstructed. A remnant of outstanding *talmidei chachamim* still remained.

But the *yeshivah* of Rashi in Troyes began to gain new prominence.

Outstanding *talmidei chachamim*, such as Rabbi Yitzchak ben Asher, who had survived the Crusades, came to study under Rashi.

Rashi was now one of the few surviving masters who had inherited the tradition of the *yeshivos* of the Lorraine.

In the summer of 1097, fully a year after schedule, the Crusaders following the direction of Pope Urban II set out. They were more disciplined and professional, and no massacres ensued.

Life slowly returned to normal.

Rashi's daughter Yocheved gave birth to three more boys following Shmuel. Yaakov would grow up to be known as Rabbeinu Tam. Yitzchak would become known as the Rivam (not to be confused with the Rivan, husband of Yocheved's sister, Miriam.) The third son was named Shlomo. All four sons would grow to become the greatest *talmidei chachamim* of their time. To this day, their profound influence on the study of Torah—in particular, the *Gemara*—permeates every *yeshivah* throughout the world.

Rashi loved his grandchildren dearly. Once, he came into the synagogue, carrying one of them on his shoulders. (*Haoraah* 2:133)

A story is told that one day, Rashi, wearing a *tallis* and *tefillin*, was holding Yaakov (Rabbeinu Tam) on his lap. The boy grabbed Rashi's *tefillin shel rosh*, and tore them off his head.

"What are you doing?" His mother ran up to him.

Rashi laughed. "When he grows up, he will disagree with me on the *halachos* of *tefillin*."

As is well-known, Rabbeinu Tam disagreed with his grandfather on the order of the *parshiyos* in the *tefillin*. (A few years ago, archaeologists discovered some pairs of *tefillin* from the times of *Chazal*. Some followed the opinion of Rashi; others that of Rabbeinu Tam.)

Meanwhile, many Jews in the Lorraine were going through a living hell. They had converted to Christianity under threat of death and torture during the Crusades. Now, according to church law, they were prohibited from returning to Judaism.

Not only were they unwilling Christians, but their old compatriots wanted nothing more to do with them. Various communities treated them like pariahs, subjecting them to humiliating indignities.

Some Jews refused to drink the wine of forced apostates. Who knows if he secretly clings to the religion of the Nazarene?

Rashi expressed his uncompromising opposition to all these attitudes.

These forced apostates, he wrote, "had their hearts toward Heaven," acting as they did only out of fear. "G-d forbid that we avoid their wine and shame them. All that they did was due to the massacring sword. As soon as they can, they will hurry to abandon their present way of life with all their might." (*Hapardes*)

179

When Emperor Henry IV returned from Italy some years after the massacres, Rabbi Moshe ben Yekusiel of Speyer petitioned him to allow the apostate Jews to return to Judaism.

Emperor Henry agreed to let these Jews resume living an openly Jewish life. This decision was met with amazement and indignation by Pope Clement III, who had succeeded Pope Urban II in 1099.

The pope wrote to the bishop of Bamberg, "We have heard that the baptized Jews have been permitted to apostasize from the church. This is something outrageous and sinful. We require you and all our brothers to ascertain that the sacrament of the church not be desecrated."

Pope Clement was not outraged by the forcible conversion of Jews to Christianity. But he was shocked that these Jews should be allowed to return to their faith. The pope was named "clement—meaning, merciful and compassionate.

Having allowed forced apostates to return to Judaism, Emperor Henry began an investigation into the murder of the Jews, culminating in the punishment of Archbishop Ruthard and his men for having profited from the property of the murdered Jews of Mainz.

In addition, he also extended the Jews under his domain the same protection offered the clergy.

But some members of the Jewish community did not welcome the forced apostates back into the community.

There was the case of a young couple, for instance, who had gotten married while in a state of forced apostasy. Now that they could again act as Jews, the community refused to honor their marriage.

When these cases came before Rashi, he protested vigorously. "Even were a Jew to become an apostate of his own free will," he replied, "his marriage would be valid—how much more in such a case, when the couple was converted by force, and whose hearts had always been with G-d; and especially since they proved their sincerity by abandoning Christianity as soon as they could."

Rashi went further. He refused to reject even those who sinned willfully. "If a man sinned by transgressing a public decree, he is still counted for a *minyan* (unless he was put in *cherem*) . . . Even though he sinned, he is still a Jew." (*Haoraah* 2:130)

"It is forbidden to take interest from an apostate Jew, for he is still included in the *mitzvah* of 'Do not take interest from your brother.'"

He went on. "Our principle is, even if a Jew has sinned, he is still considered a Jew. This refers as well to his divorce, to *chalitzah* and marriage. In all these, he is considered a complete Jew." (*Haoraah* 2:116)

Elsewhere, Rashi elaborated, "We may not divide him from the religion of Israel. It is true that he isn't to be trusted regarding *kashrus*. But his marriage is a marriage and his divorce is a divorce. In short, he is like a suspected Jew, for an apostate is like a Jew in all matters. May the Rock of Israel enlighten our eyes in the light of Torah." (*Teshuvos Maimonios, Nashim* 29)

Rashi was a man of peace.

In one region, there was a rash of assimilation. Some blamed those who were assimilating. But Rashi blamed the problem on a lack of peace among community members. "Set your hearts to pursue peace," he wrote. "Look! For our sins, those in your region have been struck with a terrible blow. As a result, they are assimilating among the gentiles. But peace will help you overcome this. Then evil will not be able to rule. As our Sages taught, 'Great is peace, which was given as part of the portion of the righteous and not part of the portion of the evil-doers.' May He, Whose name and blessing are peace, grant you peace." (*Teshuvos Chachmei Tzarfas* 23)

Rashi's respect for his fellow-Jews was expressed in his actions. Whenever he received a present from a Jew, he didn't investigate whether it might have a *halachic* problem. His attitude was that Jews aren't suspect, since they are holy. (*Haoraah* 2:110)

Out of his empathy for his fellow-Jews, Rashi was sensitive to how *halachic* decisions affected their income. He wrote, "Do not think it a light thing to cause Jews to lose money."

To meet the economic needs of the time, he made business relations with gentiles easy. "In the exile," he wrote, "we cannot do without business dealings with the gentiles, for we live among them. We earn our living from them, and we cannot afford to insult them." (*Avodah Zarah* 11b)

Rashi allowed the taking of interest from a gentile in a certain case that others had prohibited. A Jew had borrowed money from a gentile and gave an item to the gentile as collateral. The gentile in turn borrowed money from a second Jew, giving that second Jew the same item as collateral. The question now was: Is the second Jew allowed to take interest on his loan to the gentile, even though the money originally came from the first Jew? Rashi responded, "Whoever holds himself back from taking interest in such a case is a pious fool." (*Haoraah* 2:123)

But in his own life, Rashi tried to avoid business dealings with gentiles.

Once, when a gentile owed Rashi money, Rashi decided to frighten the gentile into admitting his debt. Rashi told the gentile that they would go to the church, and there the gentile would swear upon a relic—the ashes or bones of a Christian saint.

The gentile agreed. At the last minute, Rashi pretended to reconsider and give him more time. Rashi knew that he didn't have the right to cause the gentile to swear on such relics.

From that time on, Rashi decided not to engage in business

with a gentile unless he had a clear, written agreement. (*Haoraah* 1:153)

Rashi's students copied and collected his many *teshuvos* and *halachic* decisions. About three hundred *teshuvos* are extant.

Machzor Vitry contains material regarding prayer. It was edited by Rabbi Simchah of Vitry, whose son, Rabbi Shmuel, married Rashi's granddaughter, Miriam (daughter to Yocheved and Rabbi Meir). *Siddur Rashi*, composed by an unknown student, deals with the same topic. *Sefer Hapardes*, which includes most of the material in *Siddur Rashi*, was put together by Rabbi Shemayah, Rashi's student. *Sefer Haoraah* was put together by Rabbi Nassan Hamachiri of southern France. (*Sefer Issur Veheter* by Rabbi Yosef ben Yitzchak and *Sefer Hasedarim* are mostly duplicated in the books mentioned above.)

19

Godfrey of Bouillon

OVER THE PASSAGE OF YEARS, A TALE WAS TOLD ABOUT RASHI AND Godfrey of Bouillon, one of the leaders of the first Crusade.

A draft rushed through the damp castle chamber, and the flames behind the hearth sizzled.

Duke Godfrey entered the large room, his hair still wet from the hot bath, and went to stand before the fire.

"Dinner!"

"Yes, my lord!"

Two serving men scurried out of the room and returned with bread, milk, eggs and fish.

Godfrey sat at the table and tore into the bread. "Where is Jean-Francois, my musician?"

"In bed with tuberculosis, my lord."

"A pity. How about my Italian musician, Michelangelo?"

"He has been having ecstatic visions, my lord."

"How is that, footman?"

"He had eaten of the damp rye bread, my lord. Many have noted that Heaven favors those who partake of it with mystic clarity. Perhaps it is due to the ergot mold."

"Yes, well, never mind," he said, slopping a soft-boiled egg into his mouth, half of which dripped down his beard. "How about my musician, Jean-Luc?"

"Jean-Luc!" the footman bellowed.

A short, hunched man hurried into the chamber, gripping a lute. "Here I am, my lord!"

"Play for me one of your fables, Jean-Luc!" Godfrey commanded.

Jean-Luc sat upon a stool, strummed upon the strings and began to sing.

> "*Un loup et un aigniau enmainne*
> *Soif, pour boire a une fontainne . . .*"

A wolf did drink at flowing creek
And said to lamb, "Don't even speak.
I see that you, your dirty feet,
All matted, sweated with the heat,
Have muddied all my water."

The lamb replied, "Oh please, kind sir,
The water's muddy since you stir
It with your paws. But I'm downstream
From you, and would not dream
To meddle with your water."

The wolf then said, "You wretched lamb,
What sort of fool d'you think I am?
Such words, you wretched little fool,
Might gain you friends in flock or school—

Not here down by the water."

The wolf went on, "I know your kind,
I know your heart, your thought, your mind.
Six months before, your father here
Also, in his foolish cheer,
Muddied up the water."

"That's not my fault," the sheep, forlorn,
Replied. "Back then I was not born.
And so, dear wolf, you stretch too long
To claim that I have done you wrong
And muddied up your water."

"Ah, so you say," the wolf replied.
He snatched the sheep. "I think you're snide."
He shook him in his jaw, then sighed.
"I'll have to eat you, since you've died,
Here beside the water."

The moral that we may infer
Is that the wolf won't have to stir,
For if he's hungry, he'll produce
Any kind of lame excuse
To kill down by the water.

                (*Mishlei Shu'al* and other sources)

"Bravo!" Duke Godfrey exclaimed. "Of course, such a character has nothing in common with me!"

"None, my lord." The musician bowed low before the duke and scuttled out of the room.

"Servant!" exclaimed the duke.

"Yes, my lord!" The serving man leaped forward.

"Allow the Jew, Rashi, before me!"

"He is not here, my lord."

"Not here?" Godfrey took hold of the serving man's nose and twisted it, so that he bent a knee to the floor.

"You shall break my nose, sir!"

"I told you to get Rashi!" Godfrey flung the serving man backward, and he flew into the grate before the fire.

"Rashi refused to come, my lord. He said you were an evil man, begging your pardon, and that he would not come before you."

Godfrey grabbed a silver trumpet and pressed it to his lips. He blew a stirring clarion call, and five generals entered the room. They saluted and stood at attention before the duke.

"We begin our march for Jerusalem at dawn!" Godfrey declared. "And we'll make a stop over on the way at Rashi's *beis midrash*."

"Aye aye, sir!" The generals saluted, turned on their heels and marched out the door.

The next morning, an immense army swarmed across the earth of France, marching eastward toward Jerusalem.

At mid-day, they came to the *beis midrash*.

Godfrey swung off his massive charger. "You men, remain here!"

Suspiciously, he approached the *beis midrash*. All the doors and windows were open. He looked inside. Nothing. He stepped inside gingerly. "Hello!" He looked in all the rooms. No one was there.

"Shlomo! Shlomo!" His voice echoed through the empty rooms.

There was a voice. "What does my lord wish?"

"Hey! Where are you?"

"Right here, my lord!"

Godfrey looked about wildly. "Shlomo!"

"Yes, my lord."

"I want to talk to you!"

"Speak!"

"I can't see you!"

"No, my lord."

Godfrey stomped out of the *beis midrash* into the damp mistral. "Is there any Jew here?" he bellowed.

A blue door from an adjoining house opened, and a small teenager came out.

"Come here, you!"

The teenager walked up diffidently.

"Listen, you! My name's Godfrey. Duke Godfrey of Boullion!"

"Yes, sir."

"Go into the *beis midrash* and tell Rashi to come to me. I swear by my head that I won't hurt him."

The student went into the *beis midrash*.

A minute later, the student came out to Godfrey and told him, "Rashi will see you now."

As Godfrey walked into the *beis midrash*, Rashi swept down the aisle toward him and bowed.

"Rise!" commanded the duke. "I have seen your wisdom and your mastery of the secret arts. Look outside the window. See! I have prepared a hundred thousand riders. And upon the wine-faced sea, two hundred great ships await me, their great white sails billowing in the salt wind.

"In addition, seven thousand riders stand at Akron.

"With these forces, I intend to capture Jerusalem from the heathenish Saracen. I hope to G-d to overcome them, for they have no understanding of the science of war. Now tell me your thoughts. Speak frankly—I shall not hurt you."

Rashi replied curtly, "You shall capture Jerusalem—"

Godfrey threw his hands up in joy.

"—And rule over it for three days."

"And then?"

"On the fourth day, the Muslims will drive you out of the

city. You shall escape by the skin of your teeth, and return here to Europe with no more than three horses."

Godfrey ground his teeth. "It may be that you speak the truth. But if I return with four horses, I shall throttle you and cast your flesh to the dogs. And then I shall kill all the Jews of France! What do you think of that?"

"The door is behind you," Rashi replied in an icy tone, pointing over Godfrey's shoulder.

Godfrey turned on his heel and marched out the door, leaving it open. A moment later, his hand appeared in the doorway. It grasped the doorknob and pulled the door shut with a clangor that shook the walls of the *beis midrash*.

As Rashi had predicted, Godfrey overswept Jerusalem, and held onto its fortifications for three days. Then, on the fourth day, the Muslim hordes poured over the walls and drove the Crusaders back. Men chopped at each other in savage combat. Blood ran from knives and swords. The glory of war!

Godfrey's hundred thousand riders were savagely slaughtered. His two hundred golden ships were boarded and set ablaze.

Scarred and weary, Godfrey rode his steed back to Europe, accompanied by three compatriots on horseback.

Four years had passed.

As Godfrey passed by the walls of Rashi's city, he recalled Rashi's prediction and his own threat. Bitterness welled in him. "I told the Jew that if I came back with four horses, I would throw his flesh to the dogs and kill all the Jews of France!"

Godfrey slapped his horse's flank with the flat of his sword. "Hiyah!"

The three men accompanying their lord rode after his galloping charger to the city gate.

As the last rider entered under the gate, a heavy stone fell from the wall. It crashed down directly on the rider, killing him and the horse at a blow.

Godfrey swivelled his horse around and walked it to the body of his long-time companion.

Now he had only three horses. Rashi's prediction had come true. For the first time, the romance of the Crusade faded from Godfrey's heart.

All that was left was the gritty road, his companion dead in the street, and the memory of a thousand wasted days and a hundred thousand lives destroyed.

He swung off his horse. "Wait for me here."

He walked slowly, disheartened. He would bow before Rashi and continue home.

He opened the door of the *beis midrash*. Tens of students stopped their learning and looked at him. He was tall, cruel-looking, his hair matted, his face streaked with dirt, his clothing torn, a sword at his side.

"Where is Rashi?"

Silence.

"Where is Rashi?" he roared.

"Begging your pardon, sir. Rashi is no longer alive."

"No longer alive?" Godfrey whispered. "I had come to pay homage to him."

Head bowed, Godfrey stumbled from the *beis midrash* into the white sunshine. He had lost his illusions about his greatness.

"Well, did you find him?" Godfrey's companions were standing next to their horses at the trough.

Godfrey looked at them with empty eyes. He drew his sword from its sheath and beat it viciously against the water trough, back and forth, until it shattered. He gazed at the broken handle in his hand, then let it drop to the ground.

His companions glanced at each other.

"He's dead. The Jew is dead."

His companions looked at each other again. One of them shrugged.

"Well, what are you waiting for?" Godfrey yelled. "Let's go!"

Outside the city, Godfrey rode by the cemetery. He swung off his horse and for a long while stood before the grave in the long grass, his hat in his hand.

Then he got back onto his charger and slowly rode away, accompanied by his two companions, never looking back.

20

Completing a Life's Work

RASHI'S SONS-IN-LAW WERE BECOMING OUTSTANDING *TALMIDEI chachamim.*

The Rivan and Miriam had a son, Yom Tov, who became a *talmid chacham.* They also had a daughter named Miriam like her mother. This girl grew up to be a respected and learned woman whose customs served as the basis of later *halachic* decisions. (*Teshuvos Deshayichi Lehilchos Maachalos Asuros*, 5, in *Mishnah Torah*) (She is not to be confused with Yocheved's daughter, who was also called Miriam.)

Rashi's grandson, Shmuel (the Rashbam), was almost twenty years old.

When the Rashbam learned his grandfather's commentaries on *Tanach*, he felt that they did not go far enough in explaining the *pesukim* in a simple manner.

The Rashbam later reported in his own commentary on the *Chumash* that he told Rashi his opinion, and Rashi deferred to his young grandson.

"In their piety," the Rashbam wrote, "the earlier rabbis were deeply involved in *derash*—which is of the essence. As a result, they weren't accustomed to the depth of the simple meaning of the *Chumash*... Rabbeinu Shlomo, the father of my mother, who enlightened the eyes of the exile, commented on Torah, *Neviim* and *Kesuvim*, devoting himself to explaining the simple meaning (*peshuto*) of the *pesukim*. I argued with him. He agreed that if he had the time, he would have to make different comments according to the understandings of *peshat* [the daily discoveries by linguists] that are being discovered every day." (Rashbam on *Bereishis* 37:2)

But the Rashbam also wrote, "He who cares about the Word of G-d will not veer from the words of my grandfather Rabbeinu Shlomo. Most of the *halachos* and *derashos* that he cites are close to the simple meaning of the verses." (Introduction to *Vayikra*)

The Rashbam also wrote a commentary on the entire *Gemara*. Unlike Rashi's commentaries, these were quite long.

Rashi, displeased with them, instructed that they not be learned. (*Chones*)

Rashi's work now began to draw to an end.

At last, he completed his commentary on the Torah. The Chida writes that when Rashi completed the commentary, Moshe Rabbeinu appeared to him in a dream and told him, "Happy are you that your commentary accords with what I received from Heaven." (*Shem Hagedolim*)

Rashi continued to work on his commentary on *Tanach*, discussing points with his students.

He wrote commentaries on all of *Tanach* except for *Divrei Hayamim*. (The commentary on *Divrei Hayamim* was apparently written by the students of Rabbi Saadiah of the Rhine, who incorporated material from Rashi's *yeshivah*.)

It seems that Rashi left his commentaries on *Ezra* and *Nechemiah* incomplete, and that they were finished by his students.

On various occasions, Rashi would acknowledge difficulty in understanding a *pasuk* and reported that he would consult with his students to clarify matters. He wrote in his commentary on *Yechezkel*, "At any rate, I erred in that explanation, and now I learned with my colleague [student] Shemaya, and I corrected it." (*Melo Chofnayim*)

Another student who was involved in Rashi's commentary on *Tanach* was Rabbi Yosef Kara, who had first been a student of his uncle, Rabbi Menachem ben Chelbo. Rashi learned from Rabbi Yosef many things that Rabbi Menachem had said, and he incorporated these into his commentary. This was especially true of his commentary on *Sefer Yechezkel*.

Rabbi Shemaya and Rabbi Yosef edited Rashi's commentary on the Torah as we have it today. Apparently some of their own notes and additions were incorporated into the commentary.

Rashi's commentaries on the *Gemara* were also reaching their final form. A clear commentary on the *Gemara* was especially needed now that the Crusades had destroyed the *yeshivos* of Lorraine.

Rashi had revised the commentary twice before. What now exists is the third edition. The commentaries were not brought to a complete close. Rashi's son-in-law, Rabbi Yehudah ben Nassan, supplemented the commentaries on *Makkos* (after 19b) and commented on *Sanhedrin* (*Chelek*), and possibly *Nazir*. Rabbi Shmuel ben Meir commented on *Pesachim* (after 99b) and *Bava Basra* (after 29a).

Rashi was exacting in his commentary. Rabbi Yitzchak of Vienna, author of *Or Zarua* (twelfth-thirteenth centuries) saw actual manuscripts in Rashi's own handwriting. Rabbi Yitzchak wrote, "I learn Rashi's commentary with great care. I saw the commentaries that he wrote with his holy hand. At first he wrote one thing . . . then he erased it . . . and wrote something over it with a mark and wrote in the margin . . . and then there was another word written and erased, which I couldn't make out." (*Or Zarua* 1:61)

Incidentally, the well-known "Rashi script" in which Rashi's commentaries is written are not the script that Rashi himself used. "Rashi script" is a font that was first employed by Italian printers in the late 1400's when printing his commentary, because in "Rashi script" many words can be squeezed onto a line while still leaving the print easy to read.

The great, inspired commentaries were at last drawing to a close. Rashi's amazing abilities, his divine inspiration, his ability to encapsulate in a phrase the wisdom and brilliance that other commentators would have needed paragraphs to express, were set down for all generations to come. Their apparent simplicity, their depth, their genius, their accessibility to all were universally appreciated.

Yet beyond all this, there is still a quality that such descriptions cannot do justice to. Rashi's commentaries breathed the spirit of the Torah itself.

21

Rashi's Partner in Heaven

FOLK TRADITION TELLS A TALE ABOUT RASHI IN THE CLOSING YEARS of his life.

Rashi walked slowly home from the *beis midrash*. On the black street, a warm, lazy breeze rustled the leaves above his head.

An hour earlier, the heavens had poured down rain like a tent spilling out its water, and the drops now whisked down from the sky. As Rashi stepped into his house, he thought of his life. Had he come to the point where he could take joy in knowing that he served G-d in all ways?

Rashi stepped into the house silently.

Yes, he thought, when he considered his life and all that he had accomplished, he must acknowledge that he was assured a place in Gan Eden. But who, he wondered, would be his partner there?

196

Slipping off his shoes, Rashi stepped into the other room.

With the voice of the nightingale rustling like silk outside his shutter, Rashi drifted into sleep.

Then he was standing before a voice that spoke to him. "Avraham ben Gershon Hatzaddik of Barcelona will sit at your side. He shall be your companion in Gan Eden." There was a vision of a thin man with noble features and a long beard, learning and serving G-d. Rashi blinked open his eyes.

The sun was pouring light into the white-washed room. From the other room, he heard the clink of china.

Rashi washed his hands and stepped into the other room. "Listen, my wife. I must travel to Barcelona to learn of my partner in the hereafter."

She looked up at him, a dish in her hand. "Shall *I* not be beside you there?"

"I must see who shall be my *chavrusa*."

The journey to Barcelona, at the end of spring when the rains had already fallen, was a mosaic of farmers under the lemon sun, geranium petals, swarms of fleas in the luminescent blue air. Roads led through villages where barns overflowed with plenty and to towns just miles away where people sat in the road, bellies distended with hunger.

The salty smell of the sea air blew through all of Barcelona, blazing white under the Mediterranean sun.

"Where does the *tzaddik* Rabbi Avraham live?"

The fisherman squinted at Rashi. "No such person!" He went back to cutting the marlin.

At the grain store, where large pellets of barley and wheat were heaped in burlap bags: "Where does the *tzaddik* Rabbi Avraham live?"

"Never heard of him. Will you buy some grain? Excellent quality!"

In the *beis midrash*: "Where does the *tzaddik* Rabbi Avraham live?"

"Rabbi Avraham? There is no Rabbi Avraham here!" This from a small, thin man with a pointed beard.

"Are you sure you have the right address? Barcelona in Spain, right?" And a burst of laughter—from two teenagers sitting in a corner.

"Very well," Rashi said. "Where does Avraham ben Gershon live?"

The man with the pointed beard looked Rashi up and down. "An honored man like yourself? What do you want with him?"

"Meaning what?"

"Meaning to say, he is no *tzaddik*, friend. He is a wealthy man, an aristocrat who cruises the Mediterranean for sport, removed from the community. Is it him you have come seeking from the northern lands?"

"Perhaps I can help."

"If you think so . . . At any rate, I shall tell you where he lives."

Rashi walked along the narrow lane of rough stone, scintillating white. He heard a teacher's voice as he walked beneath a tree in whose branches green linnets chirped.

Avraham ben Gershon's house was a silver palace with white stone towers from whose parapets flowed crimson banners. Before the dazzling towers, servants beneath a red and white, pointed canvas roof were setting up a buffet. The scent of smoked fish and cognac mingled in the hot breeze.

At the gate, a crowd of poor people gazed on hungrily in dusty rags.

Musicians tuned their instruments, and the faint notes blew toward them. A clown somersaulted through the air and leaped up, white-gloved hands outstretched, smiling delightedly.

Rashi called through the gates to a servant. "I wish to speak to Don Avraham!"

"A moment!" The servant, in white shirt, black pants and vest, put some crystal on the table and went into the castle.

Rashi's thoughts drifted to Avraham ben Gershon. He thought of those who are given their reward in this life, because they do not deserve . . .

A tall, distinguished aristocrat came up to the gate—the man Rashi had seen in his dream.

"Jiminez, let this man in!"

The servant opened the gate and allowed Rashi to slip through.

"You wished to see me?" Avraham's smile was deep.

"I see you live a wealthy, lordly life," Rashi said.

Avraham smiled. "I enjoy, as the foreigners say, 'the good life.'"

The two men strolled on the blue-green sward. Servants and maidservants hurried past. Lords and ladies were gathered in small claques, murmuring.

"Is this the sort of life that G-d desires?" Rashi said.

"There are many ways to please Him."

"G-d desires the heart!"

"Fasting and weeping are not the only way to serve Him." Avraham picked up an hors d'oeuvre from a table beneath the gay tent. He muttered a blessing and popped it into his mouth. "Have one!"

A servant appeared. "The paupers are murmuring at the gate."

"Today I will go deal with them myself. My heart is glad, for tomorrow my daughter shall be wed."

They passed under the rippled purple, half-transparent banners of the tent.

At the gate, Avraham distributed golden coins to the outstretched hands of the paupers, who thanked him.

"I suppose you shall marry your daughter to a wealthy suitor?" Rashi said.

"In fact, I am marrying her to a poor young man."

The paupers had dispersed, hurrying back to the market. Only one poor woman remained, clutching her ragged shawl and weeping.

"What is it, my good woman? Here is a coin."

She shrank back. "I have not come to request money. I seek advice."

"Speak." In the sky, crows passed like a cluster of stones.

"I am a widow who works hard to raise my children. My young daughter, Bilhah, got engaged to a man who I thought would give me grandchildren. But he has been blinded by wealth and abandoned my daughter."

"What is this of which you speak? And why have you come to me?"

"I am telling you that the young man has abandoned my dear daughter to marry a woman of wealth. And I come to tell you these matters because it is *your* daughter that he intends to wed tomorrow!"

Avraham furrowed his brow.

"What shall you do now?" Rashi asked. "Surely you shall give this widow's daughter some money and make an end of the matter."

Avraham only said to the woman, "Come back tomorrow."

Rashi passed the night in Avraham's palace, next to a room in which were collected birds' wings, nautilus shells, dried rattlesnake grass, driftwood, fan coral, maidenhair fern. An artist working at an easel looked out at Rashi, a pixyish expression on his face.

The next day, the palace was filled with an extraordinary bustle. Guests appeared at every moment, riding up to the gate in carriages; attendants dashed about, carrying trays and tuxedos; the bride flitted nervously through a room, her face veiled, two maidservants rushing after her, make-up in their

200

hands; servants with silver platters of food hurried to the banquet hall.

Only once did Rashi see Avraham, who had a pleased expression on his lips, pursed as though he were keeping himself from laughing.

Why should such a man be his companion in Gan Eden?

The *chuppah* was set up, the guests gathered. The bride entered, her face covered by a heavy veil. The groom stood beside her beneath the *chuppah*.

His fingers opened a small box and took out a golden ring.

She put her index finger out.

He looked carefully at the ring. With one small sentence, he would change his life forever.

With one small movement, he would no longer be alone, half a human being, a bird with one wing broken.

"Behold, you are betrothed to me . . ." He slipped the ring on her outstretched finger.

Avraham whispered something to the rabbi. The rabbi nodded. Avraham leaned forward and lifted the veil from the bride's face.

The groom looked into the eyes of his new wife—and his mouth opened. "Bilhah!"

"What—"

"What is it?"

The room exploded into pandemonium. The groom's parents started yelling. His father grabbed Avraham's lapel. "What's going on?" Guests turned to each other. "It isn't Don Avraham's daughter!"

"Quiet!" roared don Avraham. "Silence, right now! Listen to me, good people. I learned yesterday from a poor widow that her daughter was engaged to be married to a boy who loved her dearly. But under great pressure from his parents, he broke the engagement and got engaged to my own daughter for her wealth. When I heard this, I knew that I could not allow it to be. And so today, I switched brides.

"I am sure that my daughter will find someone worthy of her. But today, let us celebrate the wedding of this young man to the woman he was meant to marry.

"And so, let us celebrate!"

He waved an arm at the wedding band, which struck up a tune.

Rashi rushed over to Rabbi Avraham, embraced him and kissed him on his cheeks. "Now I see that you are fit to be my companion in Gan Eden! Today, you have made me happy."

Rashi remained with Rabbi Avraham for the length of the *sheva brachos*, which Rabbi Avraham arranged for the poor couple.

Then he journeyed back to Troyes. Travelling at dusk, he remembered the words of the song that the townspeople had sung: "Under my feet, the moon glides along the river." He was growing older; his beard was entirely white. How many more full moons would he see reflected in the water? One day soon, he would pass from this world into the next, like a man stepping from one room to another.

22

In Purity

RASHI LAY IN BED TOO WEAK TO EVEN RAISE A HAND. ONE OF HIS
daughters sat at his side, and he dictated to her a complex
teshuvah regarding *issur veheter*. "Here I am . . . condemned
to the suffering of disease, lying in my sickbed. I have no more
strength, and my hand cannot even pick up a pen. And so I am
dictating these lines to my daughter." (*Shivlei Haleket*)

(There are those who claim that Rashi dictated to one of
his grandsons. The phrase, *v'lachein, biti karasi*—"and so, I
dictated to my daughter"—can be read, if one of the letters is
changed, to *ul'ven biti karasi*—"and I dictated to my daughter's
son.")

Other times, Rashi dictated to his students. "His strength
waned, and his mouth could not speak of all the troubles that
passed over him, wave after wave, as a result of which his
hand grew too weak to write . . . And so he dictated *teshuvos*

to his students, who wrote." (*Teshuvos Chachmei Tzarfas* 15)

Like his grandsons, Rashi's granddaughters were outstanding people. As mentioned earlier, Miriam, daughter of his Miriam, served as a model for determination of *halachah*.

Yocheved's daughter, Chanah, was said to teach other women laws and customs relevant to women. (*Otzar Nechmad*)

Rashi also continued dictating his commentary on the *Gemara*.

Rashi lay in bed, his pale, wrinkled hands on the bedcover. It was the twenty-ninth of *Tammuz* 4865 (July 13, 1105). At his side, sat his son-in-law Rabbi Yehudah ben Nassan, holding a sheaf of parchments. He read to Rashi from his commentary on *Makkos*. Occasionally, Rashi interrupted in a soft voice to make a correction or add some words.

Rabbi Yehudah read from the text of the *Gemara*.

Rashi shook his head. "That isn't the right reading," he said.

Rabbi Yehudah leaned over to hear better.

"The correct reading is in the *Sifrei* . . . The *pasuk* says, 'After he washes in water, he becomes pure.' After he immerses himself, he can eat the *maaser*."

Rabbi Yehudah wrote down Rashi's words. There was a long silence—very long.

Rabbi Yehudah looked up.

Rashi lay still in bed, his eyes unseeing.

Rabbi Yehudah rushed to Rashi's side and took his hand. It was soft and inert. Rashi's eyes looked out blankly.

His pure soul had left his sainted body with words of purity upon his lips.

Rabbi Yehudah later continued his work on *Makkos* from the point where Rashi had passed away. He wrote there, "Our Rabbi! His body was pure. His soul left in purity, and he explained no more. And from here onward continues the language of his student, Rabbi Yehudah ben Rabbi Nassan."

Rashi's students mourned: "Taken is the ark of G-d, the holy of holies, the advisor and wise speaker, the great teacher, our Rashi, son of the holy Rabbi Yitzchak of France, in 4865, 29 *Tammuz*, at the age of 65." (*Siddur Rashi*)

"Just as the date tree owner knows the proper time to pick the fruit," another mourner wrote, "so did G-d know the time of Rabbeinu Shlomo. He took him at the proper time, to seat him in the Heavenly *Yeshivah*. Woe, he is no more!—'for G-d took him.'" (Manuscript Farma, Rashi on *Iyov*)

Rashi did not have any sons. But when he died, tradition tells, a voice called out from Heaven, "In the future, all Israel will be your sons." (*Heichal Rashi*)

Rabbi Menachem ben Zerach wrote in his *Tzeidah Laderech*, "Before the time of Rabbeinu Shlomo, the great teacher of Troyes, people used to learn with the commentaries of Rabbeinu Gershom Meir Hagolah, which were very long. The holy spirit rested upon Rabbeinu Shlomo, and he grew strong in Talmud. He composed commentaries in a clear, short language—the first such commentary of its kind, which enlightened the paths of the sea of the Talmud."

Avraham ibn Ezra was the first person to call Rashi "Parshandasa." He wrote of Rashi's commentary on the Torah, "A star has come down from France . . . like Shmuel from Ramah. He has enlightened the blind. Whoever is thirsty for honey drinks of his sweetness. He has composed an awesome commentary on the Torah. Therefore, he is called Parshandasa. His book enlightens all who have questions, and he is desired by Israel . . ." (Parshandasa appears in the book of *Esther* 9:7, but it can be read as an Aramaic phrase: Interpreter of the law.)

The first known sefer to be printed in Italy was Rashi's commentary on the *Chumash* (without the text of the

Chumash), published in 1475.

Rashi's commentary on the *Chumash* was even renowned among Christian academics.

Nicholas de Lyra (1292-1340), a French Franciscan, made great use of Rashi's explanations in his work, Postillae Perpetuae. So closely did he follow Rashi that he was nicknamed Simius Solomonis—the ape of Solomon.

The Ravan (Rabbi Eliezer of Mainz), who learned with Rashi's son-in-law and grandsons, wrote of a *teshuvah* of his: "His *teshuvah* is laden with raisin cakes and golden apples, with plates of silver and gold . . . His lips were filled with knowledge and Torah . . . The Torah of truth was in his mouth. He walked in peace and straightness and set up a third foot for the world." (Before, the world was like a stool that only has two feet: *Mishnah* and *Gemara*. But now the stool could stand, for Rashi added a third foot: his commentary.)

Rabbi Yaakov of Moyres, one of the *Baalei Tosefos*, had a question about three *halachos* (in *Rosh Hashanah* 20b). He didn't know whether to follow the explanation of Rashi or that of Rabbeinu Zerachiah Hagadol. In his sleep, he put his question to the Heavenly Court, and he was answered, "What is this that you have rushed to find, my son? The verse says, 'There has shone in the darkness light for those who are straight.'" (*Tehillim* 112:4). In the Hebrew, this can be read as 'Zerachiah (*zarach*) is in darkness; there is light for Rashi (*yashar*—the letters of Rashi.)'" (*She'elos Us'shuvos Min Hashamayim*)

The Sh'lah wrote, "Rashi wrote his work with the holy spirit. It must be studied carefully, for in one word he would hint at great insights."

23

Even After His Death, A Tzaddik Lives

RASHI HAD PASSED AWAY. BUT STORIES WERE TOLD OF HIM IN Heaven and how he appeared to *gedolim*.

Rabbi Eizik of Kamarna told Rabbi Yitzchak Eizik of Zhiditshov that when Rashi died, his soul rose up to Heaven, where it was met by the entire Heavenly Family.

"Make place for Rashi!" they cried.

Only the angel Metatron did not come out to greet Rashi.

Metatron had lived on earth as Chanoch. The *Chumash* tells that "Chanoch walked with G-d."

Rashi had explained, "He was a *tzaddik*, but it was possible that he might return to do evil. Therefore, G-d hurried and made him die before his time."

Metatron was very unhappy that Rashi had not written that G-d had brought him up to Heaven alive like Eliyahu and transformed him into an angel.

Rabbi Yitzchak Eizik of Zhiditshov replied, "I will defend Rashi's words.

"Why did he say, 'return to do evil'? He should simply have said 'return to evil.' But the word *leharshia*—to do evil—can also mean 'to make someone else do evil.'

"Chanoch was a *tzaddik*, but he was too quick to incriminate the rest of the world, to assume that they are evil—which they were, in comparison with him. Rashi should be read, 'He was a *tzaddik*, but it was possible that his judgment would bring down an accusation against the rest of the world that they are evil.'

"This is similar to the story of the woman of Tzarfas whose son died after Eliyahu visited her. She told Eliyahu, 'Until now, I was righteous in comparison with the people of my city. But in comparison with you, I am not considered anything. And so when you came, you made my sin stand out, and my son died.'"

Rabbi Yitzchak Eizik of Zhiditshov concluded, "Now, let Metatron declare, 'Set aside a place for Rashi!'" (*Maasei Vesichos Tzaddikim*)

One night, Rabbi Chaim Vital (student of the Arizal) wrote, Rashi came in a dream to his grandson, the Rashbam, and woke him up.

"Who are you?"

"I am Shlomo, your grandfather. Rise and wash your hands, and learn from me how to read G-d's hidden Name, for I have taught you everything except this."

The Rashbam did as his grandfather requested. He sat with Rashi, although he didn't see him, and Rashi taught him.

Finally, Rashi said, "Understand the explanation well, for I do not have permission to remain any longer." (*Megillas Sesarim*)

When Rashi had been alive, he had not wanted to teach this secret to the Rashbam. He waited until he learned in

Heaven that the Rashbam was indeed worthy of learning this secret, and he received permission to teach him. (*Shem Hagedolim*)

Rashi has his own *yeshivah* in Heaven. The Maharsha of Belz taught that whoever learns Rashi on the *parshah* every week is guaranteed that when he goes to the world-to-come he will be admitted into this *yeshivah*. (There may be higher *yeshivos*, but he is at least promised that he will be allowed to enter this one.) (*Sefer Divrei Yitzchak*)

Rabbi Yehoshua of Cracow, author of *Pnei Yehoshua*, also composed *Meginei Shlomo*, in which he defended Rashi's commentary on the *Gemara* from the criticisms of the *Baalei Tosefos*.

Rabbi Yehoshua's grandson told that Rashi appeared to Rabbi Yehoshua in a state of joy and told him, "Happy are you in this world, and you will do well in the world-to-come, for you saved me from the mighty lions, the *Baalei Tosefos*. When your time comes, I and all my students will come to welcome you into the world-to-come."

When Rabbi Yehoshua lay on his deathbed, a half hour before he passed away, he was surrounded by the great *talmidei chachamim* of Cracow.

"Make a space for Rabbeinu Shlomo who enlightened our eyes," he called out. "The *gaon*, Rabbeinu Shlomo Yitzchaki has come to me with all his holy ones. They are receiving me with joy to show me a path of life, because I always stood at his right side to defend him against the questions in the *Tosefos*." (*Kovetz Rashi*)

Similarly, it is told that Rabbi Eliyahu Mizrachi merited to see the face of Rashi because he defended his commentary on the Torah from the comments of the Ramban. (*Moznei Tzeddek*)

Rabbi Ezriel Aryeh Leib wrote a work called *Shleimah Mishnaso*, defending Rashi's comments on *Berachos*. He told his son that one night when he was working on this *sefer* in the town of Amtzislav, he fell into great sorrow because he was unable to answer a sharp criticism against Rashi. Rashi appeared to him in a vision and began teaching him, and he wrote down Rashi's words. (Introduction to *Shleimah Mishnaso*)

Gedolim showed the greatest respect for Rashi's commentaries.

Once, Rabbi Levi Yitzchak of Berditshev was invited to a *seudas mitzvah* celebrating the *siyum* of a *mesechta*. This took place during the "Nine Days," when ordinarily one could not eat meat.

Rabbi Levi Yitzchak asked the man making the *siyum*, "Can you assure me that you didn't skip even a *laaz*—a foreign word—in Rashi?"

"No," the man replied.

"In that case," Rabbi Levi Yitzchak replied, "I am afraid that I will not be able to join you for the meal."

Once, a *melamed* came to Rabbi Yisrael Meir Kagan, the Chafetz Chaim, and asked him for a letter testifying that he is a qualified teacher.

"What is your specialty?" the Chafetz Chaim asked him.

"I am an expert in Rashi on the Torah."

"In that case," the Chafetz Chaim said, "come here and sit in my place."

Rashi is like the air we breathe. He is absolutely necessary, yet one can come to take him for granted.

Rashi the man passed away. His era has receded, and his historical conditions no longer exist.

Yet Rashi lives today as vibrantly as ever.

Some people explain the Torah and others speak for the Torah. But a man like Rashi embodied the Torah.

Like the sages of the *Gemara* or the *Geonim* after them, Rashi achieved the paradoxical ideal of the Jew: to be an individual living a worthy life and at the same time a vehicle for G-d's Will.

Like Moshe Rabbeinu, Rashi was the humblest of all men. Like Moshe Rabbeinu, he too became the teacher of Israel.

Like the school of Hillel, Rashi was modest and calm, and, like them, his words too became the words that all Jews live by.

The works of Rashi have become inextricably intertwined with the Torah itself.

Thus Rashi is the "Teacher of Israel."

Glossary

afikoman: final portion of *matzoh* at the *Pesach seder*
aliyah: honory post at the Torah reading
askan: activist
beis (batei) midrash: study hall(s)
beis din: rabbinical court
beis: Hebrew letter
bimah: pulpit
chassan: bridegroom
chassid: adherent to *chassidus*
chavrusa: study partner
chazan: cantor
cherem: excommunication
chol hamoed: Intermediate Days of the Festivals
chuppah: bridal canopy
daled: Hebrew letter
darshan: preacher
daven: pray
derech eretz: common decency
eiruv: demarcation of private domain
gabbai: synagogue president
gadol: great one
galus: exile
haftorah: supplementary Torah reading
hakafah: circumnavigation
halachah: Jewish law
kapotes: frocks
kashrus: state of being kosher
kesubah: nuptial agreement

213

kiddush: sanctification of *Shabbos* or festivals
ksav: lettering
maaser: tithe
machzor: prayer book for high holy days and festivals
melamed: teacher
mezuzah: scroll affixed to doorpost
michtav: letter
mikveh: ritual bath
minhag(im): custom(s)
minyan: quorum of ten
mishloach manos: sending of gifts (on *Purim*)
mishnah: part of the Talmud
mitzvah: Torah commandment
niggun: tune
parnas: leader
peirush: explanation
pesukim: verses
peyos: earlocks
piyutim: poetic liturgy
Purim: Festival of Lots
rebbi: Torah teacher
reish: Hebrew letter
rishonim: the early ones
rosh yeshivah: dean
sandek: one who holds the infant during circumcision
seder: Passover feast
sefer: book
selichos: penitential prayers
seudas mitzvah: feast in celebration of a good deed
shiur(im): lecture(s)
shivah: seven-day period of mourning
Shmoneh Esrei: the Eighteen Benedictions, fundamental part of daily prayers
shtreimel: *chassidic* headdress
shul: synagogue
siddur: prayer book
siyum: conclusion
tallis (talleisim): prayer shawl(s)
talmid chacham: Torah scholar
tefillin: phylacteries
teshuvah: repentance; responsum
treif: unkosher
tzaddik: righteous person
yashar: straight
yeshivah (yeshivos): Torah school(s)
yud: Hebrew letter
zman: semester